Jonathan Ross

Jonathan Ross

the unauthorised biography

NEIL SIMPSON

JOHN BLAKE

Published by John Blake Publishing Ltd,
3 Bramber Court, 2 Bramber Road,
London W14 9PB, England

www.blake.co.uk

First published in hardback in 2006

ISBN-13: 978 1 84454 262 8
ISBN-10: 1 84454 262 9

British Library Cataloguing-in-Publication Data:

A catalogue record for this book is available from the British Library.

Design by www.envydesign.co.uk

Printed in Great Britain by Creative Print & Design, Ebbw Vale

1 3 5 7 9 10 8 6 4 2

Papers used by John Blake Publishing are natural, recyclable products made
from wood grown in sustainable forests. The manufacturing processes
conform to the environmental regulations of the country of origin.

Every attempt has been made to contact the relevant copyright-holders,
but some were unobtainable. We would be grateful if the appropriate
people could contact us.

Pictures © Rex Features p1, p3, p4, p5, p6, p7, p11, p12, p14, p15; Empics
p2, p3, p5, p6, p8, p10, p13, p14, p16; Mirrorpix p9

Contents

Introduction

'And the winner is... Jonathan Ross for Friday Night with Jonathan Ross.'

It was Sunday, 7 May 2006, and Jonathan Ross couldn't stop smiling as he threaded his way across the ballroom at London's Grosvenor House hotel to collect his latest Bafta award. At the press conference, Jonathan admitted that a tiny part of him had hoped that his rival Noel Edmonds might have won that evening – like many people, Jonathan was a big fan of Noel's new show *Deal or No Deal*. But, by almost every measure you could imagine, *Friday Night with Jonathan Ross* makes for better all-round entertainment. And when you are up for the Best Entertainment Performance award, that is the only thing that matters.

Back in Jonathan's north London home, the Bafta trophy would be in very good company. Jonathan had won the same award just two years earlier, alongside just about every other major broadcasting accolade. Over the past two decades, he has become, quite simply, our favourite entertainer and broadcaster. Once we may have loved to hate him for his outrageous suits, wide-boy manner and dodgy accent. Now we just seem to love him, full stop.

So, earlier in the year, not even the news that he earns the equivalent of more than £56 a minute for his Radio Two show could trigger a backlash against him. The boy from Leytonstone, east London, is seen as the ultimate 'boy done good'. So no one seems to begrudge him a penny of his vast rewards, especially because he continues to be one of the hardest-working performers on the airwaves.

Friday Night with Jonathan Ross, the BBC1 chat show that won him his latest Bafta, is still 'must-see' television. But, behind the scenes, Jonathan has also worked hard to make it 'must-appear-on' television for celebrities at home and abroad. Nearly 20 years earlier, Jonathan's desperate phone calls had often been left unanswered when he had been touting for guests on his first show, *The Last Resort*. Today, his relentless networking means he frequently finds himself with more guests lined up than he has time for on the show. The roster of stars he attracts is also able to push all the rival chat shows into the shade. Yes, Michael Parkinson spoke to Tony Blair in 2006... but Jonathan spoke to everyone else.

What means even more to Jonathan is the fact that his other shows are enjoying the same purple patch of success. The sniffy voices who said he was too lightweight to step into Barry Norman's shoes with the BBC's *Film* strand had clearly never looked at the Jonathan Ross CV. His love of film had carried him through his East End childhood, and his passion for film trivia helped get him his first job in television.

More importantly, the film industry itself recognises Jonathan's commitment to cinema. He has become, quite simply, one of the best-connected men in the entertainment industry. That is important, because, for all their love of publicity, American stars are not always easy to attract on to British review shows, especially if the hosts are something of an unknown quantity. But Jonathan isn't just known in Hollywood, he is also respected. So whether it is the latest teenage ingénue or the most Oscar-laden old stager, they are happy to talk to the one reviewer who really loves and clearly understands their world.

When he took over Barry Norman's job, Jonathan said he would like to beat Barry's record of 26 years in the chief critic's chair. It may have seemed an unlikely dream back then, but you wouldn't bet against him achieving his goal now.

Away from the film world, what makes Jonathan stand out against all the other show hosts and entertainers is his off-the-wall sense of humour – as David Cameron discovered when he was a guest on *Friday Night With...* and was faced with a series of risque questions about Margaret Thatcher. But at the same time, Jonathan has a great ability to laugh at himself as much as he does at everyone around him. He is probably the only person in Britain who can host the *British Comedy Awards* year after year and always end up the funniest man in the room. His ability to hold an evening together and keep the talk coming means he is also the obvious choice to control long hours of live television on other major events, whether it is New Year's Eve or *Live 8*.

And for all the jokes and close-to-the-bone comments on radio and television, Jonathan also wins fans for being a new and possibly unlikely incarnation of the classic English gentleman. His marriage has certainly had some ups and downs – but it has ultimately survived and thrived. Every photograph of Jonathan with his wife and children speaks volumes about how close they all are and how good a husband and father he has become.

So how did Jonathan Ross get to be so successful – without turning into a classic showbiz monster? Until now, very few people really knew, because Jonathan has given precious few interviews about his own past, present or future. This biography digs beyond his obvious achievements to find out what those closest to him think about 'Wossie'. They include the people he has grown up and worked with, the ones who know just how tough and hard his road to the top has been.

Today, Jonathan Ross lives less than ten miles from his old childhood home in London's East End, but his real journey has been far greater. It has taken a shy short-sighted boy all the way to becoming the coolest and most confident star of British television. And it proves why the Bafta he won in 2006 is highly unlikely to be his last.

1

Party of Five

The tall thin boy with the thick, Coke-bottle glasses ran upstairs to his room and closed the door. It was crowded inside – with two bunk beds, one single bed, two wardrobes and two chests of drawers taking up almost every inch of available floor space. But at least, for once, it was quiet.

The boy climbed up to his top bunk and pulled his newest *Fantastic Four* comic out of its paper bag. When you share your bedroom with four brothers, you don't get many spare moments like this to yourself, so nine-year-old Jonathan Ross was determined to make the most of this rare moment of peace. He wanted an escape from the reality of his frantic East End childhood and knew he could always lose himself in the imaginary, technicolour world of American superheroes.

For as long as he could remember, comics had been both

a refuge and an inspiration to the desperately short-sighted and deeply shy Jonathan. And it wasn't just any old superheroes that fascinated him. He liked the ones that made him feel better about his own life and gave him a bit of confidence about his future. 'Spiderman was my favourite because he was the really skinny guy with glasses who was useless at everything until he got bitten by a radioactive spider. I dreamed something like that could happen to me and I had a whole fantasy life going on in my head even then. I always used to like the stories about superheroes with problems. I would think, "Hey, I have problems too. So maybe I can do something heroic as well."'

Born in Camden, north London, on 17 November 1960, one of Jonathan's earliest problems was simply getting noticed. He was the third boy in the family, after elder brothers Paul and Simon. They had all moved east to Leytonstone when Jonathan was two and his first younger brother Miles arrived. Their next brother, Adam, was born little more than a year later, just before the family were finally blessed with a girl, the baby of the family Lisa. With just three bedrooms (one of which was for Lisa) it had turned into the ultimate crowded house. Not surprisingly, it was almost constantly noisy as well. Neighbours, friends and other Ross relatives dropped by on a near daily basis for meals and chats, so competition for space and attention was always fierce.

Big brother Paul sums it up, giving an early clue about why he thinks each of the six Ross children would one day end up in the entertainment business. 'We're all mouthy and we all have a natural tendency to show off,' he says.

'You need those things when you have a sister and four other brothers to compete with. If you are in a big family, the way to get attention is either to throw a tantrum – and our mum and dad wouldn't put up with that – or to be engaging, funny and receptive. We went for that and it held us in good stead for the future.'

Jonathan's memories are a little different, however. As a child, he reckons he wasn't yet ready to show off and certainly hadn't awakened his dormant motor-mouth gene. 'In big families, you don't really communicate,' he says. 'There is always this big rush, this scramble, this noise and it is all happy-sounding but, at the end of the day, you're never really talking.'

And for many years, the young Jonathan felt he didn't have anything much to say. Whenever the pressure was on, he would switch off by heading back to his top bunk and burying his head in comics – becoming almost obsessed by his favourite characters and plots. Years later, he was able to really indulge this hobby and buy tens of thousands of pounds' worth of rare magazines and posters. As a child, he used to beg his parents and grandmother for any spare coins and agonised in the newsagent's over which new comic to buy with his precious funds.

When money was tight, he did have his own drawing to fall back on, though. He and his best friend Joe used to sketch superheroes in their exercise books at school and talk endlessly about plots on the way home. Jonathan even came up with a pseudonym – D'Arcy Sarto – for the dark, increasingly detailed strips he tried to draw.

'I was probably more obsessed with all that than was

healthy and, of the thousand or so comics I had or wanted to have, I could name every writer, every artist and every plot,' he says, admitting that his dad in particular was worried that his introverted middle child wasn't developing academically and didn't seem to want to grow up.

This immaturity manifested itself in other ways as well. Jonathan had been a nervous, even neurotic child, with more than his fair share of worries and issues. Already highly conscious of the fact that he had trouble with pronouncing the letter 'r', he was sometimes tongue-tied in public. And when he did have to go out, he would refuse to leave the house without his blue comfort blanket – something he grew so reliant upon that his mother had to cut it in two so he could still have a piece to hold while she washed the other half.

But, however introverted he appeared as a young boy, Jonathan always seemed ready to break out of his shell. Shy children don't normally like the idea of leaving home and going to school. But one of Jonathan's favourite early memories is of sitting on a swing in the park drinking a chocolate milkshake and being told his first day of school was at last just around the corner. He was thrilled at the prospect. And while he claims he can't remember this next incident, the older members of his family delight in reminding him about his first ever public performance.

At six years old, Jonathan strapped a baby bath on to his back and crawled naked out into the garden during a family party. He was doing an impression of a turtle, he said, even though he unaccountably roared like a lion and sat up and begged like a dog in an attempt to prove it. As surreal sketches go, it would almost have been good enough for a slot on *The Last Resort* many years later.

Mixing up his animals was perhaps understandable for the young Jonathan because the Ross household was almost as full of pets as it was of children. The first of the family's cats would frequently give birth at the end of one or other of the boys' beds. And while most of the new kittens were given away, those that remained soon had something else to deal with – the family's first puppy. Jonathan was given the job of giving him a name and he made a strange mistake in the process. What he wanted was to name the puppy Tog, after the half-dog, half-sprite from the *Watch with Mother* classic *Pogles' Wood*. What he did, though, was demand that his puppy be called Trog. 'For some reason, I couldn't seem to pronounce the word "Tog" properly so I went for the name Trog instead. It was probably the only time in my life when I deliberately added the letter "r" to a word,' he joked years later.

Having so many of his siblings at the same school meant that Jonathan soon settled into life at Davies Lane Junior School, right on the edge of the bleak Wanstead Flats. After a while, he even stopped wanting to take his blue comfort blanket with him every morning. And one day, in the late 1960s, just before Jonathan's eighth birthday, he and the rest of the family were to get a fantastic surprise when they all trooped home at the end of the school day. Somehow, their parents, John and Martha, had saved up enough to replace the family's tiny old black-and-white television with a far bigger colour model. The whole family was entranced. And a second reason why they would all gravitate towards the entertainment industry in adulthood began to become apparent.

Far from restricting the amount of television that the children could watch, John and Martha thought there were enormous benefits to be gained from the 'always on' set in the corner of their lounge. Money had always been incredibly tight, with so many mouths to feed and bodies to clothe. John was a part-time lorry driver and also worked as a boilerman in the local hospital, while Martha only had time for a few part-time jobs while the children were growing up. Big trips into the West End of London were pretty much out of the question, while adventures further afield were practically impossible. Going abroad wasn't something the family ever even thought of; Jonathan only got his first passport when he was 22. But, while John and Martha thought they couldn't afford physically to show their children much of life, they felt they could at least make them aware of the world's possibilities through the magic of television. Everyone in the family was brought up to believe totally in the power of possibilities that the small screen could provide.

'There was absolutely no snobbery about television in our house,' remembers Paul. 'Our parents regarded it as a window on to the rock-'n'-roll 1960s and on to everything else as well. If anything, we held television in elevated regard compared to everyone else we knew. It wasn't about being slumped in front of a television screen. It was about respecting the things that screen could show and teach you. We all loved television, even then. We were inspired by it from the start.'

Jonathan says his parents were equally determined that their children should develop other talents. 'Mum always encouraged us to explore things and to do what we wanted. Dad was stricter and encouraged us to read,' he says. And in the process, another vital personality trait was developed. Jonathan says he gradually became aware that his whole family was 'relentlessly self-improving'. It seemed as if, with Lisa and Adam approaching school age, and the Ross headcount finally settling at eight, the time had come for new directions. It was to be onwards and upwards for everyone and the seeds of all their future careers were about to be sown.

The first stop on this new journey was a quiet residential street all the way across London in leafy, soon-to-be-middle-class Turnham Green. It was the home of the Wendy Wisby modelling agency. 'Mum had seen an advertisement in the London *Evening News* effectively saying: "Unless your kids are hideously ugly, they could make money on adverts," so off we all went,' remembers Paul.

The child modelling world was fiercely competitive, even then. The mix of pushy parents, precocious children and demanding clients can be volatile to say the least. And the Ross family was told to expect a lot of tears and rejections if they tried to find work. In the worst-case scenario, Martha was told, she and the kids could traipse across London for an endless series of auditions and never really earn a penny in return. Other children would always be deemed prettier, cuter, funnier or more endearing. Being turned down, week in and week out, could affect even the most confident of children. It could seriously scar those of a more nervous disposition. Were the Ross children really strong enough to cope with the challenge?

Martha looked around at her brood and knew that they were. She would make sure they knew the nature of the advertising business – that rejections were business, not personal. And, anyway, she was convinced that very few rejections would come their way. My family's gorgeous, she told herself. How can anyone think they won't win every job they go up for?

Back in Leytonstone, an urban myth about a former neighbour was also spurring Martha on. It centred on John Hewer, who had been picked as the original Captain Birdseye in the food company's commercials and who had built a whole showbusiness career on the back of it. He had gone to the same local school as most of the Ross boys. So Martha was hoping they could follow in his footsteps – and, as it turned out, she was almost entirely right. All six of her children were signed up to the Wendy Wisby agency after their first interview and the work soon started to come in.

One of the first big jobs the whole group won was to play happy families in a big-budget Persil advert. Jonathan joined the rest of the family on a subsequent shoot playing with a huge St Bernard dog in a Winalot commercial, and did a campaign on his own for Rice Crispies. For more than three years, the family kept on the advertising treadmill. Cereal, milk, insurance, shampoo – they auditioned for jobs promoting all of them. And, between them, they seemed to win more than their fair share of work.

Fortunately, all the early fears that too many rejections

might scar the children for life turned out to have been misplaced. On the contrary, the Ross kids thrived on the whole process of the work. They had no problem differentiating the business from the personal. They liked getting to know other children at group auditions and were easy to amuse even during long, potentially boring shoots. Perhaps most tellingly of all, they felt that walking into a photographic studio or on to a commercial set was like entering their own private Narnia. They were being given a look behind the scenes of the worlds they watched on television at home, an early insight into a world most of their school friends knew nothing about.

The Ross children also saw first-hand just how much easy money there was to be made in the advertising and entertainment world. Working on a television advert could pay as much as £8 a day – which may not sound like much today but was nearly half the average weekly wage for adults at the time. 'It made a huge difference to the family finances and all of us caught the showbusiness bug doing the shoots,' says Paul.

Jonathan, in particular, found that the auditions and the shoots gave him a vital confidence boost. Being in a central London studio, miles from Leytonstone, gave him a rare sense of freedom. And not even a few high-profile rejections could take this from him – at one point, for example, he and his brothers lost a lucrative Ribena advert to another dark-haired child model who would also end up in the public eye; his name was Michael Portillo.

Back at school, this newfound confidence was becoming obvious to Jonathan's teachers. He had entered a competition in the *Blue Peter Christmas Annual* which had asked readers to guess how many words had been said on the programme in the previous year. After agonising privately for days, Jonathan realised he didn't have a clue. But, instead of giving up, he picked a number almost at random and sent it in. He didn't win, of course, but, like everyone else who entered, he was sent Biddy Baxter's signed letter of congratulations and a badge. 'It wasn't the real *Blue Peter* badge but that didn't stop me getting my headmaster to read the letter out in school assembly and insist that it was,' says Jonathan, happy for once to find himself willingly in the limelight.

Over the next few years of Jonathan's childhood, his on/off love affair with being the centre of attention would swing back and forth almost with the seasons. At auditions and on advertising shoots, he tended to be happy as the star, but much of the rest of the time, he liked to stay in the background. One reason for the return of his shyness came from his clothes. As a tall child who wore hand-me-down clothes from his shorter, elder brothers, he reckons he spent most of his childhood in trousers that ended far short of his ankles and shirts that never quite made it to his wrists. Fortunately, his parents managed to stop all the youngsters from getting jealous about who was bought what and who had to do with second best. Which was just as well. 'With five boys in one tiny bedroom, it would have been Armageddon if we had fought,' says Paul.

Martha and John had cleverly conjured up a real camaraderie among their children – though they might not have always been so happy if they had known what the six of them were doing when they went out to play. Pleased that they were happy to stick together in one big gang, Martha and John didn't always ask many questions about how they all spent their afternoons. It was years, for example, before they found out that they would often indulge in the highly dangerous game of chicken at Leytonstone railway station, where the last to run in front of an incoming train was the winner.

Fortunately, no one got hurt on the train tracks, although family life with the Rosses was never entirely incident free. At different times, Paul, Miles and Lisa were all involved in minor car accidents, respectively suffering severe bruises, a broken collarbone and hairline fractures of the skull. On summer evenings and at weekends, the gang would take long walks with Trog – on each side of Leytonstone, the long streets of terraced houses give way to the two open spaces of Hackney Marshes and the Wanstead Flats. They weren't exactly Royal Parks but, for city children who craved adventure, they were hard to beat. Jonathan, always feeling like a middle child with so many siblings both above and below him in the family pecking order, was keenest on these outdoor adventures because his imagination ran riot as they played. He imagined he was a lone cowboy on some final frontier. He wanted to be a hero on his own personal film set. Films, even as a child, meant a huge amount to the East End boy – and even today he can map out much of his early development against them.

At just six years old, Jonathan remembers being wide-eyed and star-struck when his dad took him to Leicester Square for the first time. They saw *2001: A Space Odyssey*, the biggest box-office draw of its day. When he was ten, Jonathan remembers sneaking downstairs to try to watch *Psycho* on television. And, at 13, he found a way to slip through a fire exit to watch the X-certificate *The Exorcist* in the local cinema. As it turned out, he soon regretted that last one, however. 'It took me about four hours to get home afterwards because I stopped at every corner and peeped round just in case the devil was waiting for me. I was terrified,' he says.

Cinema also gave Jonathan most of his childhood heroes and role models. His biggest hero was fellow cockney Michael Caine, though not simply because of his East End background or because of the roles he played. Jonathan loved Michael as Harry Palmer in *The Ipcress File* and *Funeral in Berlin*, because he was the first film star the teenager could think of who wore glasses – and made them look cool. 'He was the first star to do that since Harold Lloyd. Like Spiderman, Michael Caine made me feel better about my own awful glasses and it was also brilliant when he took them off because then you always knew there was going to be some action,' Jonathan says.

In some ways, while Jonathan certainly didn't have cinema in his blood, it may well have been in the water out in Leytonstone. Alfred Hitchcock is one of the area's most famous sons, originally working at the Silent Film Studios just north of the Ross house on the Lea Bridge Road. Directors Ken Russell and Stanley Kubrick also went to nearby colleges, while film and television stars such as Angela Lansbury and Derek Jacobi were locals. On the wider entertainment front, celebrity photographer David Bailey was another Leytonstone boy, as were such achievers as David Beckham, Damon Albarn, Graham Gooch, Frank Muir and Fanny Craddock. In 2004, Jonathan was to team up with a former Leytonstone neighbour, television presenter June Sarpong, when he won *The Big Fat Quiz of the Year* (something he would win again the following year partnering Sharon Osbourne). More exciting to Jonathan as a teenage boy was the fact that several cast members from *Grange Hill* also lived in the area – and he and his school friends would spend hours talking about where they might be and how they could meet them.

Leytonstone also had some good schools, and the Ross parents were fiercely keen to see their children take full advantage of them. Homework, all six children say, was a serious business in their house and bad school reports spelled serious soul-searching. Jonathan went to Leyton County High School for Boys, which today is listed as one of the top 200 'friendliest schools in the country' out of the 22,000 examined by Friends Reunited. Old boys (and old girls from its sister school) are keen to get in and to stay in touch with former classmates and teachers, sending more emails and posting more contact details than any other school in east London. Probably very few of those friendly pupils remember the young Jonathan, however. The confidence he had gained as a child model seemed to disappear as soon as he walked through the gates of his secondary school – and he says his sole intention in those years was to go unnoticed and avoid the bullies. 'I was seen as studious because I wore big glasses, I was skinny and I kept myself to myself,' he says. For some boys, this was a red rag to a bull and, despite having several brothers there to defend him, Jonathan was always worried about being targeted as a swot and punished accordingly.

The one thing that obsessed most of Jonathan's schoolmates was football – and with Leytonstone almost exactly halfway between Spurs and West Ham, there was a near constant battle of loyalties in the playground. Jonathan's almost total disinterest in football – or indeed in any sport – meant that he wasn't able to join in with any of the heated conversations about White Hart Lane or Upton Park. And, apart from his one friend Joe, very few of the other Leyton County High School boys were able to join in the conversations Jonathan did want to hold, because his hobbies were becoming increasingly obscure.

He was still passionate about *Captain America* and *Spiderman* comics, and had got over his initial fears over *The Exorcist*. So he started to watch as many other horror films as possible. Then he discovered the world of the samurai warrior. 'To a Leytonstone teenager obsessed with comic books, the whole samurai thing was gripping and an obvious fascination,' he says. 'While I didn't know much about the real history of these films, I had a burning love of East Asian cinema even then. I discovered films by the likes of Akira Kurosawa and loved them. Today, people see all those films as arty or esoteric, but to me as a kid they were simply exciting tales of stoic, grunting men ferociously stabbing away in the rain and mud at classic, if slightly foreign-looking bad guys. And these dark adventures had a palpable sense of menace, unlike the film and TV adaptations of my favourite western comic books which then were infested with slightly out of shape actors in too-tight spandex giving knowing winks.'

The young Jonathan put obscure titles such as *The Seven Samurai*, *Throne of Blood* and *The Hidden Fortress* in the premier league of his favourite films, and he says anything Japanese which involved butchered limbs and sizzling jets of blood came close. What he loved about this genre of films was the fact that you always knew pretty much what was around the next corner. The plotlines followed regular patterns and you felt a sense of achievement and satisfaction when you accurately predicted what was going to happen next.

Perhaps unsurprisingly, though, Jonathan failed to get this message across to either his brothers or his school friends. So his hobby became increasingly solitary, just like his early comic reading. Still desperately short-sighted, he would sit in the corner of the family living room poring over the few fanzines and arts and listing magazines he tracked down to try to learn more about his favourite films and their directors. In an age before even videos had been invented, let alone DVDs, satellite television and the internet, keeping up with this esoteric hobby was something of a challenge and, for a while, Jonathan felt increasingly isolated. He wondered whether it was weird to like these bloody foreign films, and whether anyone else would ever share his fascination.

As the 1970s got under way, Jonathan finally received a

confidence boost. Direct from Hong Kong came a new cultural explosion – the martial arts movie. Bruce Lee was his first hero of that era, soon to be followed by Jackie Chan, Tsui Hark and John Woo. All were huge stars for a brief period, and Jonathan finally felt part of the in-crowd at school and became a local hero for knowing so much about the latest teenage icons. And displaying the traditional characteristics of all super-nerds, Jonathan refused to let go of his obsession when the public mood moved on. When martial arts films descended into parody, Jonathan continued to champion the best of them and seek them out on solo trips down the Central Line to cinemas in the West End, Leicester Square and Soho.

Back in school, Jonathan was doing well – but not as well as he should have done. The Ross parents were still fiercely keen for their children to do better in life than they had done, so there were massive celebrations when eldest son Paul's A-level grades came in. He was the first person in the family ever to go to university and, if Martha and John were to have their way, he wasn't going to be the last. Jonathan, though, wasn't always on track to keep up the new family tradition. 'I wish I had understood that learning could be fun rather than a chore. I was bright at school and found it easy to get by without putting any genuine hard work in it,' he says.

In the mid-1970s, it was easy to feel there wasn't a lot of point in working hard, however. Recession, unemployment, a new IRA bombing campaign and wider fears over the nuclear threat were stifling ambition across the whole country. And the depression and anger that came in their wake would give Jonathan something else to focus on – punk music. As the Clash, the Sex Pistols, X-Ray Spex and the Buzzcocks hit the headlines, Jonathan was finally back in with the in-crowd at school. He started heading west at weekends to go to gigs and tried desperately to find friends who wanted to set up a band – years later, he joked that an ideal name would have been Johnny and the Self-Abusers. He also showed the first signs of his passion for fashion. 'I wore plastic trousers and winkle-pickers. My hair was spiky, greased and lacquered. I just loved the look.'

Meanwhile, reading comics had temporarily given way to building up a near-obsessive collection of *NME*s and *Record Mirror*s – and a family crisis ensued when Jonathan had to retake his O-levels after doing too little revision. As usual, Paul was held up as an example to his younger brother.

By the time Jonathan was preparing for his A-levels, Paul was at the University of Kent studying English Literature and preparing to do postgraduate research into the literary influences on Dickens down in Exeter. It was surprisingly academic stuff for a boy from a poor East End household. But Paul was thriving in his new life out of London and his stories of his wild student lifestyle were the inspiration Jonathan needed to follow suit. He revised hard for his own A-levels, got the grades he needed and started a course in Modern History at the London School of Economics.

By the time he began his student career, Jonathan felt it was time to reinvent himself. He says he grew up searching for the right role in life to play, the most suitable persona to acquire. So, at 18, the shy, quiet boy from school turned into the laidback class clown at university. 'I wasn't a very positive force in the classroom as I was a bit disruptive. I worked hard sometimes but, as soon as I got two or three good grades in a row, I would relax. I was more interested in keeping people amused in the bar, the pool room and, unfortunately for them, the classroom.'

That said, Jonathan didn't take any easy options when the final year of his degree approached. He picked a tough subject for his dissertation – an examination of German scholar and sociologist Max Weber and his role in the German Social Democratic Party between 1905 and 1914. Where exactly this would lead was a moot point, however. Jonathan still had some offbeat career dreams. He spent hours re-examining, tracing over and trying to recreate his favourite Jack Kirby *Marvel* comics – trying to work out if his *nom de plume* D'Arcy Sarto should be revived and if he had what it took to make it as a comic artist in his own right.

Realising that he didn't, Jonathan once more took a lead from his elder brother. A showbusiness career and a family dynasty was about to begin. Paul's first job after leaving Exeter with his postgrad degree was as a trainee reporter on a local paper and, in rare trips back to London, he made the family howl with laughter at how gloriously unsuited he was to the task. 'There was I, a London lad who had fought in the punk wars, spending my time reporting on agricultural shows in the middle of nowhere. It was never going to work,' he told them. So he quit, moved back to town and got the family's first full-time job in television. He was a researcher on the current event-based *The London Show* on ITV – then edited by Greg Dyke. Suddenly, Paul was in his element, and his parents and five siblings watched as he thrived. 'I was loving it. I had no fears about going out with a camera crew and asking people in the pub for their opinions or vox-popping binmen. It was an excuse to show off and the whole family realised that television was a perfect business for a group of bullshitters like us. It was the only time in history when you could earn a living with that kind of work.'

With Paul having so much fun – and looking set to earn a decent amount of money – it was hardly surprising that his siblings all wanted a piece of the action. A family road map had been drawn up and Jonathan wanted to be one of the first to follow it.

As well as his career as a child model, Jonathan and the rest of the Ross gang had been in and out of various amateur and semi-professional dramatic groups all their lives. In 1980, when he was a student, Jonathan managed to tie up his love of punk music with his passion for film – he got a job as a film extra in the bleak Hazel O'Connor music film *Breaking Glass*. Being an extra normally involves so much waiting around and boredom that many people only do it once. But Jonathan was happy to keep applying for similar work and ended up playing a young soldier in the eighth series of *It Ain't Half Hot, Mum* – his episode was called 'The Last Roll Call' and was first shown in September 1981 two months short of Jonathan's 21st birthday.

In the same year, Jonathan had passed another milestone, making his stage debut with a tiny organisation with the unlikely name of the Stud Tely Theatre Company. It put on a gory adaptation of *Beowulf* at the Edinburgh Festival and Jonathan played the part of a blood-dripping Norse hero. Going on stage killed some powerful demons in Jonathan's mind, fully exorcising some of the ghosts of shyness that had haunted his early teenage years. And he is happy to admit that, when it came to social skills, he had a lot of catching up to do. 'My dad was 18 when my oldest brother arrived. I hadn't even had sex by the time I was 18. I was still only dreaming about it,' he jokes.

One reason for his late development was his appalling eyesight – the thing he says had held him back socially throughout his childhood. He comes in as a minus nine in each eye, which means he can hardly see across a room without proper correction and, as the correction came in the form of ugly National Health glasses, he sometimes felt he would prefer to be blind than to see. 'I was like Mr Magoo right up until the end of my teens. Girls and women? I didn't know they were there most of the time, because I couldn't see them and I was far more into superheroes. My personal life was a disaster pretty much until I discovered contact lenses at 19.'

Even then, dating was still a huge challenge. Maybe it was because he had started so late; maybe it was because he was taking time to recognise the lens-wearing person that now looked back at him from the bathroom mirror. Maybe it was just because women in general made him nervous. But for whatever reason, Jonathan used to dream that arranged marriages were part of his culture so he could offload all the responsibilities of meeting and wooing women on to his parents.

Unbeknown to Jonathan, one shadowy career avenue was opening up for him as he disregarded the thought of drawing comic strips and decided to follow his brother's lead into the television industry. Students graduating with degrees in Modern History from the LSE in the early 1980s were considered prime recruiting material for MI5 – so, if the handlers had liked the look of him, Jonathan could have chosen espionage rather than entertainment as a career and ended up as a spy. Though had he taken the latter route, it is not clear if it would have been for all the right reasons. 'I was a big Bond fan and there was also a bit of "Connery wannabe" in me somewhere,' he says of his teenage and early-20-something years. 'I still treasured one of the ring watches with the diamante flip top I had bought years earlier. Unfortunately, it didn't have a high-power magnet for unzipping girls' dresses which was what I had been hoping for,' he says.

Jonathan's early political leanings may also have turned off any potential handlers at MI5. After university, he briefly joined the Bow and Poplar Labour Party, convinced that they could soften the way the country was changing under Thatcherism. 'But seeing all the petty wrangling that went on there put me off politics. Life's too short,' he said, after his interest had waned. And anyway, Jonathan had plenty more to focus on at this point in his life. He was looking for his first full-time job – and he was hoping to find his first serious girlfriend at the same time.

The job was proving to be the bigger challenge. Finding your way into the television industry can be like finding your way out of a giant maze. It can take forever, you face a lot of dead ends and sometimes you end up wishing you had never started. Jonathan felt he had a few things in his favour and he was ready to emphasise them all on his first CV. He made a lot of the child modelling jobs, which he thought proved he knew more than most about the media world. Then there were the bit parts he had played and the work he had done as a film extra. Surely that would be enough to catch a producer's eye?

Unfortunately for Jonathan, it wasn't. His CV was one of dozens that arrived on producers' desks every day in the mid-1980s. And in those four-channel days, there were a strictly limited number of hours to be filled and shows to be made. What made matters worse was that only a tiny minority of television jobs were ever advertised. It really was a case of who and what you knew – so Jonathan tried to pull in some favours. Paul was still on *The London Show* while their mother Martha was also in the industry, having won a role as an extra on the very first episode of *EastEnders*, a role she was to keep for more than two decades. But no one could actually help Jonathan open any doors. They just gave the same advice – write more letters, ring up more people, keep plugging away and keep your fingers crossed. Offering to do work experience for free was another suggestion – anything to prise open that door into the industry.

Swallowing his pride, Jonathan followed every instruction to the letter – and finally got an interview with an independent production company which had designs on the embryonic 'youth television' market. The company was Soho-based RPM Productions and Jonathan was taken on as a researcher for its flagship show *Loose Talk*. What he learned, pretty much from day one, was that television researchers are on the lowest rung of the entertainment ladder. Like runners in the film business, researchers really are expected to make tea, do deliveries and run the most basic of errands for the production team they serve. And they need to do it all with a smile, because none of them knows when they might be chosen for something better. 'Researchers need to be tenacious, ambitious and determined just to get taken on, and you certainly can't be a wallflower if you want a promotion,' says production manager Alice Price, who has worked for many of the Channel 4 production companies that competed for work alongside RPM Productions. 'If you think it was competitive getting the job, then you normally find that was nothing compared to the atmosphere inside the office. Huge numbers of stars started off as office-based researchers, so producers do tend to keep an eye out for who on their team shows talent. As a researcher, you never know when you might be under examination – so you need to project the right mix of being charming, confident and humble. You need to be "on" all the time.'

Fortunately for Jonathan, being 'on' was no longer a problem. Having been immersed in television all his life, he was so pleased to be part of the industry that he couldn't have hidden his enthusiasm if he had tried. He did, however, manage to hide the fact that he took a while to get the hang of the nuts and bolts of his new role. 'At the start, I didn't have a clue what I was doing as a researcher. I was always on the phone talking to my mum and pretending it was David Bowie's agent,' he admits. But, as his confidence grew, he found that working on *Loose Talk* suited him down to the ground. The show ran for two series on Channel 4 between 1983 and 1984 and was a rough template for everything Jonathan loved about life and contemporary culture.

Hosted by Steve Taylor (who had begun his working life on *The Face* and would go on to set up *Arena* magazine and become a top design consultant), the show was a rough mix of live music, comment, chat, group discussions and youth-oriented investigative journalism.

Alongside his fellow researchers, Jonathan had several jobs to undertake behind the scenes. He had to help track down and book suitable guests, writing up brief biographies for Steve and the producers and suggesting what sort of questions they should be asked on the show. On the day of transmission, he would meet the stars at the studio entrance and look after them before and after filming. And, while *Loose Talk* rarely attracted any A-list guests, it was still heady stuff for the boy from Leytonstone who had spent so many of his weekends as a teenager trying to guess where any local *Grange Hill* actors might live.

The downside, though, was that the money was lousy and Jonathan was really struggling to make ends meet. He was also beginning to spot the common denominator that linked almost all the researchers in RPM Productions and all those at rival firms that he had started to socialise with in the evenings – they were all ridiculously overqualified for their roles.

'It is hard to imagine any other industry where the people making the tea or going out in the rain to find taxis for their bosses will have first-class honours degrees and possibly even postgraduate qualifications,' says Alice Price. 'But, in television, it is accepted that you have to brush all your past achievements under the carpet and act as if picking up a presenter's dry cleaning is the gig you have been waiting all your life to win. The upside to it all is that you have plenty of other people in exactly the same position whom you can bitch to about it all after work because television is also one of the most social and incestuous industries you can imagine.'

Hanging out in bars in Soho and the Channel 4 paradise of Charlotte Street was certainly a revelation to the 22-year-old Jonathan. He hooked up with his first serious girlfriend, and briefly moved in with her, although the relationship ended amicably soon afterwards. Journalist William Leith first met Jonathan back then and reckons he was about to try out yet another new persona as his search for his true identity continued. The child model, the film nerd and the class clown had all been discarded. The role of the television insider was his latest incarnation – and Jonathan wanted to play it his own way.

Many of his fellow researchers made a virtue of dressing down to try to look cool. Jonathan did the opposite. Wearing his brothers' hand-me-downs for so many years had put him off casual or ill-fitting clothes for life. He looked through style magazines and liked the sharp, smart look of the city slicker's suits. Despite working out that he earned less than the office secretary, he decided to try to copy his new role models – and he never looked back. 'I wear suits because they make me feel more confident, more special. I actually feel better when I am dressed formally because it gives me one less thing to worry about. If I am dressed formally I can relax, because I don't have to be fashionable,' he said in his early days in the television industry. Little did he know that he would soon create a mini trend of his own when he finally went in front of the cameras.

Working in central London also gave Jonathan a chance to develop one of his new passions – trivia. He would scour the bookshops on Charing Cross Road for obscure books, magazines and facts. He loved the tiny comic shop he found near Tottenham Court Road and the music shops in Soho. On weekends, he would wander round the stalls and shops of Camden, where he had been born, looking at second-hand junk and collectables and wishing he had some more cash in his pocket.

Fortunately, this love of trivia and lowbrow culture was paying dividends at work. It gave Jonathan's comments an edge when the team was asked for new items to cover on the show, or new trends to examine. So, while *Loose Talk* was never a huge ratings success, Jonathan's job was secure. He moved on to spend another couple of years working on two other Channel 4 shows, *Soul Train* and *Trak Trix*, and also did shifts on equally unmemorable shows like *Solid Soul*.

Like most of his fellow researchers, Jonathan was fascinated by the new generation of comedy shows that were dominating the youth and cult television market in the mid-1980s; *Saturday Live* was the most influential. Ben Elton, Stephen Fry, Hugh Laurie, Rik Mayall and Adrian Edmondson were the nominal stars, but the show also introduced audiences to the likes of Dawn French, Jennifer Saunders, Nick Hancock, Jeremy Hardy, Lenny Henry, Julian Clary, Josie Lawrence and Robbie Coltrane. These were the kind of people Jonathan wanted to work with, and he loved the show itself – not least the mix of comedy and music and the fact that the producers were brave enough to broadcast it live every week. So could he get a job on it?

Jonathan went out for a drink with one of his fellow *Soul Train* researchers as he decided how to approach the transfer. His colleague, Alan Marke, had become a close friend and confidant. The pair had clicked from the moment they met, both sharing a love of the same shows, the same jokes and the same lowbrow culture. But, as the evening wore on, Jonathan made a startling discovery – he was a great deal more ambitious than he had previously thought. Going from the gopher's role as a researcher on *Soul Train* to the same role on *Saturday Live* wasn't enough for him. He and Alan talked late into the night, dissecting the way the Channel 4 show was made and how it could be improved. As the drinks bill mounted up, they reckoned that they could make an entirely new show that took the best bits of *Saturday Live*, ditched the failings and included a whole lot of unique elements of their own.

That was the show the pair of them really wanted to work on. It was the show they wanted to make.

'So why the hell shouldn't we?'

Both men say they remember the exact moment when they decided they should crunch up through the gears and launch their own show. They took a third friend out for lunch, producer Katie Lander, to see what she thought. And then the trio decided to gamble. They would set up their own company, polish up their own idea and pitch it to Channel 4. They wanted to launch the best late-night chat and music show the country had ever seen.

2

First, the Last Resort

Ironically enough for a man who didn't even go abroad until his mid-twenties, Jonathan was convinced that America could provide the perfect template for the new show. Back then, all of his biggest heroes were American – they were the Marx brothers, Muhammad Ali and the little-known chat-show host David Letterman. It was the latter who would change Jonathan's life.

By the mid-1980s, *Late Night with David Letterman* had started to go from cult hit to American institution. Filmed in a cool New York studio environment, it seemed a world away from the staid and worthy chat shows that were the staple British fare. Letterman was famous for gently mocking his guests – sometimes subtly, sometimes far more openly. He was also clearly an intelligent, quick-witted man, something Jonathan felt was a real rarity in television at the time. And he was also in total control of his studio and his environment. Jonathan loved the house band, the on-screen in-jokes with the producers and camera crew, the willingness to take risks and make mistakes on air and to take the mickey out of the whole business of making a television show.

But would his sort of irreverence get lost in translation if it was replicated in Britain? And was that why no one else had tried it before? Jonathan, Alan and Katie decided to give it a go. They spent months working into the night and at weekends on the nuts and bolts of putting a show and a production company together. They also had a perfect host in mind – the comedy writer and performer Jeremy Hardy. Jonathan in particular liked Jeremy's grown-up, politically aware humour and his ability to control a crowd. But his initial approach didn't go well. Jonathan saw Jeremy at a comedy gig, followed him into the pub toilets and pitched the job to him at the urinals. Jeremy wasn't exactly over the moon at the approach or the garbled proposal. So, when Jonathan ended his pitch, Jeremy had just two words to say in return – and, as Jonathan frequently jokes, they weren't 'Thank you'. So Jonathan headed back to the bar one chat-show host down, not daring to approach Jeremy again.

Scouting out other potential presenters was proving just as difficult, even though no future pitch took place in a public toilet. The problem was that Jonathan, Alan and Katie had come up with a budget of no more than £500 a show. It seemed a fortune to them, but it was nowhere near enough to persuade anyone decent to get out of bed, let alone to turn up at the studio.

'Shall I have a bash?'

In the end, in these five words, Jonathan's own television career was born. The trio's new company, Generation X, had booked studio time and a crew and were ready to film their first pilot show. But they still needed a host – hence Jonathan's sudden suggestion. Years later, a whole mythology would spring up around how Jonathan ended up in front of the cameras. When the group decided to call their fledgling show *The Last Resort*, it made a great story to say that Jonathan had quite literally been the last resort as a host, a man pushed out unwillingly from the wings and into the spotlight. The reality was a little different – Jonathan admits that the thought of being the show's host had always been at the back of his mind. 'The problem was that I had no idea if I could do it or not,' he says.

When he gave it a go, the results were mixed, to say the least. The pilot show got a huge professional thumbs-down, but Jonathan got rave reviews. So Generation X got the chance to try again. 'The pilot was so embarrassingly bad it was never shown,' says Mike Bolland, the senior commissioning editor for Channel 4 when *The Last Resort* was first being put together. 'But, despite the awful show, there was something about Jonathan, when you saw him on screen, which worked. It was obvious that he was still the man to present it. So we stuck with him.'

Andrea Wonfor, Arts and Entertainment Controller at Channel 4, was another powerful supporter. 'You couldn't help but notice Jonathan. He was charismatic, full of himself and, it has to be said, handsome. There was a sort of inevitability about him making it,' she says.

Television and pop critic Nina Myskow was one of the guests on the pilot show and she, too, said it was obvious that Jonathan was what television needed. 'He was bright, funny, charming and very hip from the word go,' she says. 'The show was terrible but Jonathan was brilliant.'

Back at the drawing board, Jonathan, Alan, Katie and their small team drew up a list of all the things everyone said had gone wrong with the show and all the ways they could be avoided or improved. And they were in a hurry, because Channel 4 had looked beyond the below-par pilot and commissioned a series. Nobody knew it then, but a showbusiness phenomenon was about to be born.

'Hello and welcome to *The Last Resort*!' On Friday, 16 January 1987, Jonathan Ross appeared on television for the first time in his latest guise as a chat-show host. He was wearing one of his brightest ties and his sharpest, confidence-boosting suits. He was sitting behind a desk with a David Letterman-inspired coffee cup and stack of papers and cue cards spread across it. His hair was long and slick, and he had a knowing smile permanently on his face. It was clear from the start that this latest persona fitted Jonathan to a T. It was also clear that he was ready to poke fun at himself, as well as his guests, and that he wasn't exactly sure how the whole show would pan out.

Actors Donald Sutherland and Amanda Burton were Jonathan's first guests, with music coming from one of his favourite bands, Martin Stephenson and The Daintees. He also had a house band – Steve Naive and The Playboys – who performed the theme music and played over the guests' arrivals. The show had a loose format of the 'big' celebrity, the topical guest and then something very different – the 'freak show' elements that took up a few minutes of screen time and grabbed some useful headlines. One of the most famous from the first series was 'The Regurgitator', who did just that with anything from razor blades to goldfish. It was brave and sometimes unsavoury stuff at the time, and its unlikely success ultimately spawned everything from *The Word*, *Eurotrash* and *The Girlie Show*.

As he closed his eyes in horror at some of the show's novelty acts, Jonathan proved he was among the very first of a new generation of presenters to realise that bad television could make good television – as long as everyone knew what was going on. His own confidence soared with every show he did and, in the process, he reckoned he had spotted a new *zeitgeist* in the media that was ripe for exploitation. Channel-hopping viewers were thrill-seekers, he realised. And, as well as being cynical and easily bored, they were surprisingly media aware. To them, it didn't seem to matter if a show was bad, as long as it was different. So he set out to be as bad and as different as he could be, without worrying about the consequences. It was exactly what the public wanted to see. *The Last Resort* really was the biggest show of its day.

'When something goes wrong, it breaks the bubble and that's good,' he says of the lessons he learned back then. 'When there are mistakes, it's not the glossy, fake world we're all bored with by now. Viewers think, "Someone's fucked up! Great!" And I think we all want to see people caught out occasionally. Take the times I did some really dreadful interviews. I'd worry about it but then find out that was what people wanted to watch. They would come up to me in the street the next day and say, "Cor, mate, that was fucking awful." But you could tell that they had enjoyed it. They like seeing me squirm like that, seeing me totally fuck up.'

Jonathan also saw that viewers at home wanted to feel part of a show. The contrivances and artifices of old no longer worked in an era when everyone wanted to be a television insider. So he referred to his camera crews by name and brought them into the shots, revealing the behind-the-scenes drabness of the studio just beyond the glossy set. Media studies students went wild about him 'deconstructing the genre' of conventional television. Jonathan just thought it was funny.

Back at home in Leytonstone, his family were stunned at the transformation in their once introverted brother. The television cameras seemed to bring out the very best in him. And all of them were convinced that there was much more to come – even though they were ready with a few jokey asides to keep his feet firmly on the ground. 'The camera loves some people. It loves Jonathan, even though in the flesh he is Quasimodo,' said Paul. 'I knew, as a producer, as soon as I saw Jonathan on television, "That's a TV star." There is something about certain people and there was always that thing about Jonathan. He was always deeply potty, but engaging and funny, too.'

What his parents liked was the fact that the boy who had made do with second-hand clothes throughout his childhood had certainly scrubbed up well on screen. For his part, Jonathan said he couldn't imagine wearing anything other than what were fast becoming his trademark sharp suits and bright ties. He constantly referred to his clothes in his introductory monologues, and they often seemed to get more attention than some of his guests did. More seriously, he said the big suits were central to the type of show he wanted to present – and the type of presenter he wanted to be. 'I want to look like someone who was doing a professional, slick, grown-up, American-style show. I don't want to look like just another British youth presenter. I think you dress up to go on TV. I mean, some poor sod has paid his licence fee to watch you, hasn't he? The least you can do is make an effort. I swear I wasn't vain, it was just that I was very conscious that people were looking at me. And I liked smart clothes... I would never wear jeans and a sweatshirt on television because I hate that sort of self-conscious relaxed look. And, anyway, I'm not a jeans-and-sweatshirt kind of person.'

That said, things were far from neat and tidy in the studio when cameras rolled. On most of the early shows, discarded cue cards littered the studio and lay like confetti on Jonathan's desk as he stumbled and mumbled through the show's running order. Cues were missed, producers off camera were brought on to explain what was supposed to happen next. He was 'TV lad' – a quirky, kooky, cheeky chappie who couldn't seem to quite believe his luck at being in the hot seat. And he realised that people seemed to like him, however chaotic or crazy things got.

So, as the weeks went by, he took part in some on-screen leg-wrestling with Jerry Hall and he had loud confrontations with huge stars such as Steve Martin, Paul McCartney, Mel Gibson and Meg Ryan. With each guest, he was also determined to shake things up and force them to think on their feet for a change. 'I am sure that anyone of average intelligence can sit at home and write down the first ten questions that Terry Wogan is going to ask, say, Jason Donovan,' Jonathan said when he was asked about his own planning process. 'I want to come up with the next ten that he would never ask.'

His interview with actress Carrie Fisher was a case in point. 'Does Harrison use his tongue?' he asked after quizzing her over which of her co-stars she enjoyed kissing the most. It was real-life stuff, with real risks being taken. And, sometimes, Jonathan got as good as he gave. When actress Sarah Miles was a guest, he said, 'I understand you drink your own urine,' which was something the whole team had discussed beforehand.

'I understand you eat your own shit,' she replied.

'For once, I was lost for words... on my own bleeding show,' says Jonathan.

The music was equally offbeat. One night, Jonathan got Bernard Manning to sing the greatest hits of The Smiths. Then there was the duet with Tom Jones which was credited with dragging the singer's career out of yet another of its periodic doldrums – and the smile of sheer joy on Jonathan's face as he started hoofing with his hero was credited with making audiences fall in love with the Welshman all over again. Amidst all the slapstick entertainment, Jonathan was determined to throw in some groundbreaking, artistic and intellectually challenging moments as well. Gilbert and George, Leigh Bowery, an attempt at repackaging a supposedly cooler Donny Osmond – it was all there. Eclectic, really, did not even begin to cover it.

Looking back, commentators say that it was Jonathan's inherent gaucheness and sense of simple fun that caught the mood of the country in the mid- to late 1980s. In a world still dominated by autocues and BBC-style received pronunciation, Jonathan's unscripted east London brogue and his inability to say the letter 'r', even in his own surname, was more than a breath of fresh air. It was a whirlwind. The nickname 'Wossie' had been born and the world was changing. 'The British chat show was never quite the same again,' said the *Daily Mirror*. 'As soon as Jonathan Ross stumbled into our living rooms, it was obvious that Terry Wogan's and Michael Aspel's days were numbered.'

As the buzz about *The Last Resort* grew ever louder, the start time was brought forward from its original graveyard shift at midnight to 10.30pm, where it saw ratings pick up substantially and gain even more newspaper coverage. And television executives' fears that Jonathan couldn't work in a more mainstream slot proved groundless. For all his offbeat, off-message cheekiness, he did somehow keep the show's overall tone on the right side of the taste and decency line. Yes, it was new and brash and sharp, but there were also clear boundaries. 'It was anarchic in a gentle English kind of way, like an out-of-control vicar's tea party,' was how one critic put it. It meant Jonathan attracted a vitally broad audience – he won over the young and influential trendsetters without offending the older, more traditionally minded viewer.

By the time the first series of *The Last Resort* had ended in the summer of 1987, Jonathan Ross was a bona fide star. He had been on the cover of everything from the *Radio Times* to *The Face* and, ironically enough, he was being invited on to everyone else's chat shows specifically to chat about his own.

For a while, though, Jonathan was focusing solely on having a rest. Simply putting the show together had meant working long hours – there was certainly a lot more to the job than just rolling into the studio on the day of transmission and turning on the charm. Jonathan says he was in the office by 9.00am, at least five days a week, and frequently didn't leave until late in the evening. The team worked weekends as well, as they tried to iron out the show's rough spots, while Jonathan, Alan and Katie had the extra responsibilities of ensuring that their production company had been set up properly and was running smoothly. Dealing with his sudden fame piled on the pressure for Jonathan and, while he refuses to cry the clichéd tears of a clown, he admits that behind the scenes he was nowhere near as happy as he looked on camera.

'I was totally inexperienced in the studio and every day that we filmed I panicked. I was paralysed, sick with nerves and in a fairly consistent state of worry, a permanent state of semi-anxiety,' he admits when talking about the first series. 'The show was deemed a success pretty much from the start but it was really quite an unhappy period for me.'

Potential girlfriends didn't seem to care, though. And, while their interest was amazingly flattering to the boy who had worn thick National Health glasses and had been unable to secure a date until he hit 18, he soon realised that there was a less than savoury undercurrent to his newfound popularity. 'I got a lot of attention from women, which I had never had before, and I couldn't work out why it was happening. Then I realised it was all because of my being on television and I found that rather off-putting. So I was very wary of women again, for a long time.'

That said, as an ambitious young man, newly famous and suddenly cool, it was hard to resist all of the temptations put in front of him. So, just after the first few *The Last Resort* shows had been broadcast, Jonathan was first in line when someone on the production team suggested a night out at Stringfellow's. A Page Three girl was throwing a birthday party and the bar was expected to be open (and free) 'til the early hours. It was the kind of extravagant showbiz event that Jonathan could only have dreamed of attending when he was a kid in Leytonstone. So he leaped at the chance to experience it all first-hand. As it turned out, it was less than a week before Valentine's Day and love already seemed to be in the air. Jonathan was just about to meet a precocious young pop reporter called Jane Goldman.

3

Lady Jane

There is a lot of fun to be had behind the dark smoked-glass doors of Stringfellow's nightclub on London's Upper St Martin's Lane. The dancers, the waitresses, the other partygoers – everything felt exotic and exciting to Jonathan and his colleagues as they trooped inside in search of adventure. For Jonathan, the extra thrill came from having his name on the door's VIP guest list – a first since he had become famous with The Last Resort.

In the low lights of the club's interior, the booze was flowing and everyone decided to mingle. None of the Generation X crowd really knew who the Page Three girl was, but most of them wanted to find out and all of them were superb at networking, so it didn't take long before they were all acting like old friends.

As the hours passed and the drinks continued to flow, Jonathan finally noticed two new arrivals at the party. One of them was a beautiful young woman wearing a grey

John Galliano dress and playing with her bright-red waist-length hair. She certainly wasn't the most overtly sexy woman at the party – and, like most of the other female guests, she was totally upstaged by the Stringfellow's dancers and waitresses. But something about her kept drawing Jonathan's eye. He looked at his watch. It was nearly 3.00am and, if he was going to talk to her, he should probably do it soon.

But did he have the guts? For all his bravado on and off camera, Jonathan says he still regressed into a teenage version of Mr Magoo when he had to talk to women he fancied and didn't know. And, anyway, wasn't there something ever so slightly tacky about chatting someone up in Stringfellow's? Perhaps it would be best just to forget all about it, he decided. But, as he took one last look across the bar, he realised that he no longer had a choice. The woman with the long red hair was heading straight over to talk to him. Was he blushing? Jonathan steeled himself and tried to act cool.

At first glance, Jane Goldman could not have been more different to the man she was fast approaching that weekday night in Stringfellow's. She was an only child, born into a wealthy north London Jewish family and had gone to private schools, travelled the world and enjoyed the most bohemian and privileged of backgrounds. But, for all the freedoms of her childhood, she had still acquired a steely work ethic and was renowned as the most ambitious and driven of all her former classmates. This she had proved in spades when she was taken on by the *Daily Star* immediately after her 16th birthday, making her the youngest pop writer the paper had ever employed. Still just 16, she was on duty that night in Stringfellow's – her task was to spot as many celebrities as possible, try to get some stories out of them and persuade them to come to the paper's own party the following week.

Unfortunately, the Page Three girl's birthday bash hadn't been particularly star-studded. 'I had taken a friend with me and we found there was hardly anyone there to give invitations to,' she remembers. 'Then the friend I was with saw Jonathan and said that she thought she had seen him on television the previous week and that I should give him an invite just in case, and I did. I suppose at first any attraction is purely physical and I was very attracted to him and I thought, "Oh, I hope he comes." He did, and we got talking properly then and that was pretty much it.'

For his part, Jonathan was secretly relieved when this striking woman turned out to be working the celebrity circuit when she approached him. He liked her professionalism and he recognised her ambition. And being given an invitation to a bash the following week ensured he didn't have to chat her up amidst all the topless dancers at Stringfellow's. He could calm down, prepare himself for the next party and hope to impress her then.

The following week, an extravagantly suited and booted Jonathan headed over to the *Daily Star*'s party. But, for all his outward confidence, he admits he was a mass of insecurities inside. He had no idea if this lady called Jane would actually be there. Perhaps she was just being professionally charming when they had spoken the previous week. Perhaps she was like that with every potential contact she met. Perhaps she had already forgotten him.

But, as it turned out, Jane was one of the first people he saw when he walked into the party venue. And she proved to be one of the most genuine people he had spoken to since starting out in television. They spent almost all of the evening talking – though Jonathan was happy to take a back seat every now and then when she had to head off to meet and greet some of the other VIP guests. He liked the way she seemed able to switch onthe professional, hard-working Jane Goldman when required, but was able to morph back into a relaxed and fun person when it suited her.

Taking the bull by the horns for once, he asked her out, just as the party ended. And she accepted. He headed back to his flat high above a busy main road in Shepherd's Bush feeling better than he had in ages. And, while he had yet another sleepless night, it was because he kept thinking about her, rather than because he was worrying about his next show. That, in itself, felt great and colleagues the next day were quick to spot his improved mood. They could tell he had met someone and everyone was over the moon for him. Or, at least, they were for a while.

Warning bells started to ring when Jonathan's friends found out one key fact about his new girlfriend – her age. So could a 26-year-old man really date a 16-year-old girl? And should he? Jonathan spent a lot of time talking it over with his friends and, after a while, he decided that they were right. However well he and Jane got on, however much they seemed to have in common, however relaxed they felt in each other's company, he decided to follow his friends' advice rather than his own instincts. He told her they should stop seeing each other. And then he walked away.

Jane says the rejection was devastating. 'When he found out about our age difference, he didn't call me for about a month, which felt like ten years. I felt like I just slept and hibernated in the dark while I waited to see if he would change his mind.'

What she didn't know was that Jonathan was feeling just as rough himself. So, after four miserable weeks, he picked up the phone and sheepishly suggested another date. 'I had missed her far more than I had ever expected, and the moment I saw her again I just felt pretty good about the world,' is the simple and heartfelt way he sums up their reconciliation.

Back in the office, he was ready to tough it out with his doubting colleagues, many of whom still had mixed feelings about the couple's prospects. 'So many people predicted some kind of Rod Stewart situation and thought our relationship wouldn't survive,' says Jonathan. 'But I already knew that Jane was only young in years, not in anything else, and that it was all the other areas that mattered. I also knew that, while I was older in years, I was hardly worldly wise. I hadn't had many really serious girlfriends at that point and, in many areas, Jane and I were very much on a par with each other.'

Jane's own view of the age gap was very similar. 'There's not actually that huge an age gap between us. Ten years is quite small these days, and I don't remember the subject ever being an issue for me. I know 16 is fairly young, but it is not ridiculously young and, anyway, Jonathan was quite a young 26, which balanced things out.'

So just what was it that made Jonathan and Jane click? At first glance, it might appear hard to fathom, especially as their childhoods could hardly have been more different. With wealthy well-travelled parents and a big north London house, Jane certainly had more space than Jonathan – both physically and spiritually. All her life, she had been encouraged to have big dreams and to put the work in to make them a reality. At her private school, King Alfred's in Golders Green, north London, she decided early on that she needed to work at a faster pace than most of her classmates. 'I pretty much always wanted to be a writer... I wrote all the time. I was so clear on the fact that I wanted to be a journalist that I asked my parents if I could go to a tutorial college to do my O levels early.' They agreed, so Jane left King Alfred's at just 13 and proved she had done the right thing by clocking up six O-levels over the next two years. What made this even more of an achievement was that Jane hadn't exactly been studying in solitary confinement at her tutorial college. Instead, she had been spending the vast majority of her time out in London's club scene – selling articles, reviews and profiles to the music press and earning a decent part-time income long before she was legally supposed to be working.

Years later, when she had her own television show and reporters started writing profiles of her, Jane was suddenly given a 'wild child' tag about those early days in nightclubs and on the London club scene, but she is quick to shout them down. 'I always dispute the wild-child tag. Yes, I was out there but I was working. "Wild child" to me says someone who is underage who is going out, getting pissed and falling over. But I had a job. That's why I was there.'

Jane was also furious over newspaper articles that implied her parents had left her to fend for herself as a teenager. In reality, her dad had frequently been waiting outside the West End nightclubs in his car to drive Jane home after she had been working or partying. And when she famously went to America as a 15-year-old to report on Boy George's tour, both her parents accompanied her. They stayed in the hotel next door, ready to lend support if required.

Back in Britain, and still only approaching her 16th birthday, Jane decided she wanted a full-time job. So she sent out a series of letters and cold-called as many editors as she could find before winning the *Daily Star* post that had led to her meeting Jonathan. Rick Sky, the paper's famous pop editor, says, 'Someone told me I should employ this girl who was really clued up on everything that was happening in the clubs. The extraordinary thing is that Jane was then still only a kid. But I was enthralled by her when we were introduced. Precocious is the word that springs to mind. I had no hesitation in taking her on. Her parents had made her very open-minded and she was prodigiously talented even at 16. She got in with all the bands of the moment and had become friends with people like Boy George and was invaluable to me. Ultimately, she became one of the best writers I ever worked with. But, most of all, she was a lovely, genuine person. Not qualities you always associate with the world of entertainment.'

But these were the qualities Jonathan recognised from the very start. And he also thought he saw some of his own introverted childhood reflected in hers. He had been too short-sighted to have girlfriends and had preferred staying at home with his superhero comics to playing football with his classmates. Jane, meanwhile, had been similarly isolated. 'I was a late developer,' she says. 'I was never one of the pretty girls, I was kind of the geeky, brainy kid instead, very intense and hard to know.'

Jonathan was the first person she had ever told about the years of low-level taunts and bullying she had endured at school and had always been desperate to hide. 'I didn't fit in on the social side,' she says of her mid-teens. 'My friends were becoming true teenagers – giving love bites and nicking beers – and I didn't want to do all that. I wanted to get out into the world and start working.'

Jonathan, the nerdy, skinny kid who had tried to spend his school years unnoticed to avoid the bullies, knew exactly what she meant. The final connection that the pair shared was the way they reacted to dating and the opposite sex. In the oversexed world of television, Jonathan was already secretly embarrassed about his low strike rate with women. Everyone else he worked with seemed to change partners more frequently than they changed channels and he was starting to despair of meeting anyone who shared his own belief in fidelity. The more Jane told him about her own experiences, the more he realised that he had finally found a soul mate.

'I'd been at a mixed school and there was a big element of pairing off,' she says. 'Although I kissed a boy when I was 13, I don't think I took any notice of that sort of thing until I was 16. I had a friend who was a few years older and we used to go out to gay clubs. I just seemed to fit in better when I wasn't at school or in a situation where I was supposed to cop off with someone. I hadn't had any serious boyfriends before Jonathan. There was one, who I could vaguely call a boyfriend, but I was young, I was going out a lot and I was very focused on wanting to work.'

But when she looked over at Jonathan, she reckoned she also recognised a true kindred spirit. And she says she knew instantly that Jonathan would be more than just a friend. It might have been 3.00am in the semi-darkness of Stringfellow's where they had met, but she was convinced she had already seen beyond the television personality's mask. 'That first time we met, we only talked for a matter of minutes. But I spoke to my mum the next day and told her that I had met the man I was going to marry. There was an innocence about him, a lack of cynicism and an infectious sense of joy that I just loved. He was shy, gorgeous, enchanting and I simply had a feeling that there was something very, very special about him. I was right.'

Jane, though, had one big admission to make before she started dating Jonathan again after their month-long break. Right back in the beginning in Stringfellow's, he had complimented her on her long red hair. She says he was equally charming about it the following week at the *Daily Star* party. And she hadn't yet had the courage to tell him that it wasn't hers — it was just a £29.99 hair extension she had bought as a joke on the day of the Stringfellow's bash. 'Our whole relationship was based on a lie. In reality, it was love at first hairpiece,' Jonathan joked with friends years later. But, at the time, he was still serious about getting closer to the 16-year-old who fascinated him.

'Do you want to come in and see my comic collection?'

It was hardly one of the most romantic of lines but, outside his Shepherd's Bush flat on one of their earliest dates, Jonathan knew that it just might work. Jane, he had found out, had shared his childhood love of comics. She knew all the characters and the brands, all the writers and the artists. She, too, had sat alone at home as a child, dreaming of superheroes and plotting her own primary-coloured adventures. For years, Jonathan had hoped that he might one day meet just such a friend who would share his interest – by his mid-twenties, his comic collection was already several thousand strong and included dozens of rare and valuable items. The thought of meeting a beautiful woman who had the same fascination was like winning the lottery.

He and Jane might have come from entirely different backgrounds; they might have been brought up in entirely different families, living quite different lives. But, standing in the noisy west London street, Jonathan felt they already seemed to connect and to match each other. They seemed to fit well together. And it turned out that Jane did indeed want to go in and see his comic collection.

Jane didn't end up spending the night at Jonathan's on that occasion, though. She was still living at home with her parents in Hampstead and headed back there with yet more stories about how great this new man in her life seemed to be. Perhaps fittingly, bearing in mind's Jonathan's obsession with cinema and the way his career would work out, a film was central to the first full evening he and Jane did end up spending together. But, as Jonathan admits, they certainly weren't smooching on the sofa in front of a classic romance like *Brief Encounter*, *Love Story* or *From Here to Eternity*. 'That vital evening, I enticed Jane back to my flat with the words, "I've got a bootleg copy of *Re-Animator*." It was a very violent horror movie about corpses being brought back to life. I think we only watched about 15 minutes of it before nature took its course. That had nothing to do with the movie... it was proximity on the sofa and youthful high spirits. But that film will always mean a lot to me.'

Once the couple had started to sleep together, Jonathan began to lay the foundations for his status as the ultimate one-woman man. He says he reckons the desire to settle down was somehow in his DNA. He hadn't lost his virginity until he was 21 and had slept with precious few women afterwards. One-night stands, in particular, had always been pretty much off limits. 'Promiscuity just wasn't for me. I don't think I would have been able to handle it at all. I needed a relationship. I think sex is better if there is a connection, though I admit I am saying this from a comparative position of ignorance,' he says openly.

His commitment to Jane was to be sorely tested, however. His fame on *The Last Resort* was starting to boom, just as he started to get serious with her. He was young, handsome and funny. He was a celebrity. And a near-constant stream of attractive young fans – including a handful of men – had started to make advances on him. 'I think I was aware enough to know what I could have done if I had wanted to. But I was wary of the whole idea. I somehow knew I didn't want all that. And I had Jane, who already meant so much more to me.'

Anyway, with so many other incredible new experiences on offer as a celebrity-about-town, sex with strangers was always going to be secondary to Jonathan. 'When I met Jane at Stringfellow's, I had only just discovered that I could get into nightclubs for free and that people would give me free booze and be very nice to me all night long. Believe me, all that was exciting enough.'

But Jonathan soon realised that having a proper, full-time girlfriend was even better. He and Jane tried to see each other as much as their busy workloads allowed – sometimes just squeezing in a quick early-morning breakfast in a west London café on the days when both knew they would be working late into the evening. But, while Jonathan's colleagues had overcome their initial doubts over the couple's age gap, Jane's fellow workers were still ready to scupper the love affair.

The pair had taken a quick holiday in France and, when she got back to the office, Jane found out that, in the dog-eat-dog eat world of national newspapers, no friendship can ever be considered totally sacred. One of her colleagues – she never found out who – stole her holiday photographs out of her desk drawer and put them on the front page of the paper. 'When I started going out with

Jonathan, working there was a conflict of interest, to say the least,' she says.

And the woman who had just been named 'Britain's Youngest Achiever' by *Cosmopolitan* magazine found her career was under threat in other ways as well. Questions were raised as to whether the big showbusiness stories Jane broke were leaks from Jonathan and his colleagues. Her own skills as a news reporter were suddenly being challenged. The *Daily Star* was becoming an increasingly difficult place to work for her.

Deciding to cut her losses and move on, she applied for and got a job on *Just Seventeen* magazine – neatly enough, just as she turned 17 herself. Her unique fashion sense was already turning heads – not least Jonathan's. So she decided to focus on fashion rather than pop writing and, as well as all the usual one-off features and interviews, she was given a weekly clothes column, 'Front Line'. Things went well for a while, but Jane says she soon started to spot some now familiar tensions in her relationships with the rest of the staff. Once more, just like at school, she felt on the outside looking in. 'I always felt that people saw me differently because of Jonathan. I wanted to muck in and be one of the gang, but I felt isolated. I felt, "Oh no. I don't fit in again." So I left to go freelance.'

As part of that transition, Jane made her first set of television appearances, presenting the 'Fashion Frolics' strand of the BBC1 show *Going Live* every Saturday morning – where, ironically, she was achieving higher ratings than Jonathan had got for his early episodes of *The Last Resort.*

Away from the office, Jane's other challenge was meeting and winning the approval of the whole Ross clan up in Leytonstone. Eldest brother Paul is the first to say it wasn't easy. 'There is a great closeness between all six of us kids. For us boys, any girlfriends coming into the family must have found it overpowering and pretty hard to deal with.'

And fitting into that noisy, crowded house in Leytonstone was particularly tough for an only child like Jane who said mealtimes there were like nothing she had ever seen before. Fortunately, she did have one important ally – Paul's girlfriend Kerry. As one of five brothers and sisters, Kerry was more than able to cope with the boisterous six-strong Ross clan. And she was ready to try to help Jane do the same, not least because she wanted another female around at Christmas and on other testosterone-filled get-togethers.

It was just over six months after Jonathan and Jane had got back together and started dating properly that he was given a dream trip to America to film some short interviews and vox pops in Hollywood. Staying in a fantastic hotel, seeing the Hollywood sign and getting waved into some of the biggest film and televisions studios there was fantastic. But Jonathan realised he was nowhere near as happy as he had expected to be – because he was missing Jane so much. They spoke on the phone every day, but somehow that wasn't enough. As he headed out in the unrelenting Californian sun for his final day's filming, Jonathan tried to put his thoughts in perspective. Was this puppy love? Was it just a phase? Was he blowing things out of all proportion because he was so inexperienced about relationships? Or was it the real thing? Trying desperately to focus on his work, Jonathan was convinced it was the latter.

Jane was flying out to meet him in Los Angeles the day after the work part of Jonathan's trip ended. As they left LAX and headed over to his hotel, half seriously, half in jest, Jonathan swallowed hard and asked, 'So when am I going to marry you?'

Jane's reply was equally flippant. But both knew the genie was out of the bottle and marriage was in the air. They had a wonderful week in California, where they realised they were both obsessed by theme parks and surf shops, and flew back together tanned and happy.

Every couple's first proper holiday is a test. Jonathan and Jane knew they had each passed it with flying colours. But would Jonathan raise the marriage question again now they were back in Britain? As it turned out, it took him four more months of agonising and worrying, not least because he wanted to be totally certain that Jane would say 'yes'. He needn't have worried. Jane didn't think twice before accepting, even though she admits the whole idea of getting married so young would never have seemed likely in the past.

'As a teenager, I had thought about marriage, as much as anyone ever does at that age, and decided that I would wait until I was about 30 and have children when I was about 35. But then I met Jonathan and – I know it sounds sappy – but I knew he was the right person and there didn't seem any point in waiting. We were convinced getting married early was the right thing for us to do and never panicked about it at all. We were right,' she says of the decision.

But, as an unconventional couple, they were never going to be happy with a conventional MGM Production wedding. So, instead of booking a local church, the couple booked plane tickets – they wanted to tie the knot in Las Vegas. The wedding took place just two years after they had first met and the ceremony cost the equivalent of just £30. Jonathan's Best Man was his comic-loving childhood friend Joe, who was given an original *Spiderman No 1* comic as a thank-you gift for his support.

Both Jonathan's and Jane's parents were there as witnesses and, despite the heat, the bride and groom encouraged everyone to dress up – and wear hats. Walking hand in hand around the casinos afterwards (which, strictly speaking, Jane was still too young to enter), the pair were ecstatically happy. Their shared sense of humour was already well developed and they had a fantastic time people-watching, hanging out in diners and karaoke bars, and tracking down kitsch presents for friends back home.

Las Vegas suited their love of the absurd and the ridiculous and helped cement their lifelong love affair with America. That said, they had one other honeymoon trip planned after a second party back in Britain. This was in France, where they stayed in a wonderful and expensive hotel Jonathan joked was marred only by the fact that it didn't have a television in the bedroom. The carefree joy of this second honeymoon was also somewhat interrupted by a call from Jonathan's agent in London. A Sunday tabloid had apparently been approached by a rent boy with a client who signed his cheques 'Mr J Ross'. 'Could that be you?' Jonathan's agent asked him nervously over the phone.

As it obviously wasn't, Jonathan and Jane were happy to laugh at the typical tabloid excess from their French hideaway. Little did they know that, in a decade's time, a whole new set of tabloid headlines would be even worse. On honeymoon, they had never been happier and were desperately looking forward to their future lives together. But, back in Britain, they were about to find out that living in the public eye wouldn't be nearly as easy as it looked.

4

Chat Spat

The second, hugely successful series of The Last Resort ended in the autumn of 1998 – and Jonathan felt that doors were opening all around him. Overwhelmed by the attention, he was ready to race through almost all of them. 'When someone is hot in television, they are very hot. And when you effectively take a cult late-night show into the mainstream like Jonathan did, you're the hottest,' says producer Sarah Milner, who was a researcher on his first show and has since worked with everyone from Clive Anderson to Caroline Aherne. 'Everyone will want a piece of you and everyone will be offering you new shows. The money will make your eyes water and saying "no" will be almost impossible, even if you know in your heart of hearts that some of what you are signing up to do will be rubbish.'

For Jonathan, still sometimes feeling like a lowly outsider from Leytonstone, the extra pressure was that he had no idea of just how long he might stay in demand. The man who loved feeling he had his finger on the pulse of popular culture knew full well just how quickly a trend could end. He knew his moment in the sun could cloud over at any point. So he wanted to make hay while the sun still shone, and Sarah Milner sympathised with him. 'Everyone in television is effectively a self-employed freelance,' she says. 'You feel you are only as good as your last job and, if you don't work, you don't get paid. So, when big money offers are on the table, it is very hard to turn them down just in case you never get so lucky again.'

In an ideal world, Milner says, new stars need to pick the projects that reflect their personalities or interests so they build firm foundations for the rest of their career. Fortunately for him, Jonathan got an immediate chance to do just that. Channel 4 had latched on to his lifelong love of obscure film – and so *The Incredibly Strange Film Show* was born.

What makes this show stand out, nearly two decades later, is Jonathan's bravery in making it. From the start, he refused to compromise on the directors and producers he wanted to focus on. Of the six half-hour profiles he filmed, only two, Russ Meyer and John Waters, were likely to be known to viewers, and even then to just a minority of them. The others were so obscure that some viewers apparently thought the shows were spoofs. But, despite the commissioning editor's doubts, Jonathan was convinced that the world did, in fact, need to know more about Herschell Gordon Lewis, the man who had made the likes of *Scum of the Earth*, *Color Me Blood Red* and *She-Devils on Wheels*. Jonathan also wanted to explain his obsession with Las Vegas-based martial arts and zombie filmmaker Ted V Mikels. And the man behind *Debbie Does Dallas*; Jonathan wanted the chance to profile Ray Dennis Stecker as well. So he stuck to his guns, refused to pick more mainstream subjects and ended up being proved right.

The show – riding the new wave of strangely titled programmes – was a better-than-expected ratings success. And so, the following year, he was commissioned to film another six shows under the *Son of the Incredibly Strange Film Show* banner. This time, the one big name in Jonathan's sights was Jackie Chan, while his other profiles were typically offbeat and obscure. The critics, however, loved it. 'In each show, Jonathan was again at his geeky film-buff best. He was clearly thrilled to be talking to his childhood heroes and desperate to get the message across about what he thought was so good about their films,' says media studies lecturer Paul Wallace. 'It was a pleasure to watch someone who genuinely cared about what he was reporting on, rather than just seeing a generic talking-head presenter reading out a script that had clearly been written by someone else. At that point, it looked as if Jonathan Ross could be about to blossom into one of the most influential film critics in the country.'

As it turned out, this wasn't to happen for nearly a decade, when Barry Norman decided to defect from the BBC to Sky. But, in the meantime, Jonathan was never far from the cinema, or the video rental shop. At home, he and Jane continued to love Russ Meyer and John Waters films and, at work, he constantly tried to come up with new programme ideas that could get him closer to his cinematic idols. The powers-that-be decided that something along the lines of *Grandson of the Incredibly Strange Film Show* would be a series too far. So, instead, Jonathan pitched the idea for some one-off profiles under the *For One Week Only* title.

He got the green light and put out feelers to interview the likes of *The Elephant Man* and *Blue Velvet* director David Lynch, who was enjoying new hits with *Wild at Heart* and *Twin Peaks*. Spaghetti Western-maker Alejandro Jodorowsky was also in Jonathan's sights, as was the Spanish director Pedro Almodóvar whose breakthrough movie *Tie Me Up! Tie Me Down!* had just been released. All said 'yes' to the interviews – so once more Jonathan found himself being paid handsomely for travelling the world and making programmes he would almost have done for nothing.

The good news was that he could suddenly afford to take on a few vanity projects – because he was still both in demand and in the money. *The Last Resort* continued to be the cornerstone of his career and would ultimately run for four full series. But Jonathan was busily adding several other strings to his bow.

In the early 1990s, he agreed to write a weekly comment column for a Sunday newspaper (while being the subject of a tame and false version of the kiss and tell story from one of his very few former girlfriends in a rival newspaper in what was turning out to be the new rite of passage for every modern celebrity). He did television adverts for *Evil Dead II* (because he was a huge fan of its director as well as for the money) and for *Sky* magazine as well as a couple of lager brands. He started what would be a lucrative and long-term career doing voice-overs for radio and starred in yet another television advert, this time for NatWest bank. He was asked to host a few editions of *Summertime Special* and headed to Scandinavia to film a holiday spot for *The Travel Show*.

Among a host of other spin-off activities, he put his name to *Go to Bed with Jonathan Ross*, a woeful spoof book that purported to tell the story of Jonathan's childhood and early career dreams. And he had a painted-on, big cheesy grin for a photo shoot to advertise a home computer above some toe-curlingly written prose. 'Jonathan Ross demands the best,' the advert proclaimed. 'Designer suits. Designer shirts. Designer ties. So, when he wanted a PC, it was hardly surprising he chose the Macintosh SE because, like Jonathan, it is stylish to look at, very, very productive and extremely versatile.' Embarrassing? It certainly was. But, in the celebrity stakes, Jonathan was still like a kid in a candy store – he was cashing in, enjoying everything, agreeing to almost everything and, increasingly, starting to appear on everything.

His first big variety-style show after *The Last Resort* ended was a Sunday-night venture for Channel 4 called *An Hour with Jonathan Ross*. It was billed as a mainstream mix of celebrities, chat, quizzes and music but Jonathan wanted to mix up the frothy stuff with some more serious interviews with politicians, authors and religious figures as well. Quite what the MP and the vicar thought when Jonathan gave away a pair of Elvis's well-worn trousers as a quiz prize was never ascertained, however. Jonathan had several of his showbusiness friends on hand to lend support. Vic Reeves, Bob Mortimer, Paul Whitehouse and Charlie Higson were all ready with sketches and scripts and all the usual Wossie razzle-dazzle figured in the run-up to the show's launch. But somehow, though, there was something missing when the cameras started to roll. 'It didn't quite work,' Jonathan admitted afterwards, unable to this day to say exactly why. 'It was actually boring. By the end of the hour, even I was bored.'

Fortunately, Jonathan was able to put it down to experience. Television bosses still had faith in 'Wossie' – the man who was already starting to turn himself into a brand and whose name alone could get a programme made. As Jonathan became increasingly confident in himself, as well as in his on-screen persona, journalist William Leith said the lines between the two had long since blurred. 'The point about Jonathan Ross is that there is now no difference between the person you see on TV and the TV star in real life, no difference at all. Walk around with Jonathan and you begin looking for where the camera is. He never slouches. He walks TV tall all the time. He projects his voice. Many of the things he says are clear and self-contained enough to stand a chance of not being edited out, of making it to the final version.' If anyone had ever been born to be on television, then it was Jonathan, Leith concluded.

And in the crazy days after the first two series of *The Last Resort* and his film shows, it wasn't just television that wanted some of his reflected glory. Radio stations were also lining up to get him on board.

Jonathan had first walked into the BBC's Portland Place headquarters in 1987 when he was on the crest of his *Last Resort* wave. He had been asked to take over DJ Janice Long's show for two weeks while she was on holiday; he was terrified and excited in equal measure. What bothered him was the need to learn a new skill in super-fast time. Fooling around on live television when things went wrong wasn't as bad as you might think, he said, because you could act your way out of trouble. If things go wrong on radio, though, you can't put things right by throwing cue cards around or striding out into the audience. Every mumble, every stumble, every 'um' and every pregnant pause would be magnified a million times over. And he was never sure if he would be able to time his record introductions to the second the way Janice and all the other professionals seemed to do. Back then, the cardinal rule of radio was 'Never talk over a singer'. And Jonathan was far from convinced that he wouldn't keep breaking it.

First-day nerves aside, the obvious benefit of radio was its enforced anonymity. For two weeks, it wouldn't matter what Jonathan wore or what he looked like. And sitting behind a radio mike would connect him to his comedy heroes – the likes of Tony Hancock and Kenneth Williams, who had worked in the same building a generation earlier.

As it turned out, Jonathan's two-week stint on Radio One didn't give rise to any gaffes or disasters. In fact, it won him a powerful new fan – Richard Branson, who immediately gave him a lucrative job on his own radio station, the forerunner to Virgin Radio. It was also while sitting behind the radio mike that Jonathan met someone else who would become a big part of his future. He was a young, proudly spectacle-wearing man with a mop of ginger hair who worked in the production gallery on the other side of the studio's glass screen. He was Chris Evans, a teenager in a hurry who would give Jonathan a passion for radio that would never leave him.

That passion was soon to be tested on an entirely different show. Jonathan hadn't signed an exclusive contract to any radio station, so he was free to head back to the BBC if he chose. And the offer Radio One made him in 1990 seemed impossible to refuse. The idea was for *The Jonathan Ross Radio Show* – a one-and-a-half-hour Friday-night show to be broadcast live from Ronnie Scott's jazz club in London. 'The BBC has very kindly given me enough rope to hang myself with,' he joked nervously just before the first show. 'This is going to be like nothing you have ever heard before. It will probably turn out to be impossible to listen to.'

With more than 300 club-goers in the audience for each broadcast, Jonathan knew that failure would be a very public thing. The live crowd meant that the supposed anonymity of radio had been relinquished. Yet every mumble and stumble would still be broadcast loud and clear to the nation. So Jonathan wanted to be absolutely sure that the structure of his new show was sound. Just as he had done with *The Last Resort*, he looked to America for a format that would see him through... and he found one. 'It is going to be rather like the old 60s shows in America and I'll be ringing people up all around the world and making use of the advantages peculiar to radio.' That included stand-up comedy, audience participation, interviews with the likes of Jack Nicholson (a huge coup for the debut show), and performances from buskers Jonathan selected from the Soho streets just outside the venue and 'of-the-moment' bands such as Del Amitri.

As it turned out, the drive-time 6.00pm show didn't set the world alight. But it had an unexpected effect on its host. Jonathan realised that going on radio – especially with the BBC – had forced him out of his culty Channel 4 comfort zone. It had made him feel that he could win over different, more mainstream audiences. Less than a decade earlier, he had been a painfully shy, incredibly short-sighted teenager who had hardly dared to dream that he could end up on television and had never thought he would host his own eponymous shows. But the more shows he filmed and recorded, the more confidence he acquired. Television had, quite literally, changed Jonathan's life. The boy who had been too nervous to put his hand up in class in case everyone looked at him was now in his element as the centre of attention. It was an extraordinary turnaround and proof that facing down your demons can permanently oust them from your life. And, having beaten his, the flashly suited, expensively booted, contact lens-wearing Jonathan felt ready for a host of new challenges. He wanted to know if he could win over more than the minority audiences on Channel 4. He wanted to see if he could persuade Middle England to love him.

To find out, Jonathan knew he had to get a show on either BBC1 or ITV. Back at home with Jane, he drew up the next stage of his career battle plan. And he had the biggest name in British television in his sights.

Terry Wogan had been the BBC's king of chat since 1985, when Jonathan was still working as a lowly researcher on *Solid Soul* and *Trak Trix*. The Irishman's flagship show, *Wogan*, broadcast three times a week, was central to the BBC's entire schedule, and attracted guests from princes and prime ministers down. Funnily enough, the show had also given yet another Ross brother his first piece of national television exposure – long before Paul and Jonathan made it on to the Beeb, their youngest brother Adam was playing guitar in Adam Ant's band on *Wogan* in the show's first year.

Jonathan, however, decided he would rather host the Irishman's show than simply appear on it. So, in early 1990, he put the word out via his agent that he would be interested in doing some of Terry's holiday cover – a job first taken by Kenneth Williams and latterly handed over to *Nationwide*'s Sue Lawley. And, as it turned out, the BBC were ready for a change. Terry Wogan had a holiday booked, Sue was unavailable and so Jonathan won his first primetime television slot. Jonathan's thoughts immediately turned to how he would cope with the challenge, and whether the ratings would go up or down.

Turning up at the Shepherd's Bush studios where the show was filmed, Jonathan admitted he was nervous – not least about his language. 'With an early-evening show like *Wogan* on BBC1, I can't be as rude as I normally am and it wouldn't be right to try. But it won't be easy to remember that in the middle of an interview, especially if things get heated or I start laughing too much,' he admitted.

But, while he was prepared to watch his tongue, Jonathan wasn't going to make many other concessions to the BBC code. 'I'm not selling out and I'm not changing my style because I couldn't do a po-faced interview if I tried. I'm best at high-speed comic interviews with my tongue firmly in my cheek. That's my way and that's what I'm planning,' he said after the final *Wogan* rehearsal as he looked out across the soon-to-be full theatre where it was filmed.

And, coming out of his dressing room later that same day, he proved he wasn't compromising on his image either. He was wearing a wildly clashing set of colours and his favourite Thierry Mugler jacket and Comme des Garcons socks were nothing like anything Terry, Sue or even Kenneth had ever worn on the show before. What audiences didn't know was that there was another difference between Jonathan, Terry and the others – the size of their pay packets. As the man of the moment, Jonathan had been in far greater demand for this role than he had originally realised. The BBC had wanted him badly and the bosses were prepared to pay top dollar to get him. And industry insiders said the £10,000 a week he collected for the holiday cover was more, pro rata, than Terry himself was earning.

When news of this leaked out, it only enflamed a situation that had already started to get out of control – a perceived personality clash between Jonathan and Terry. Newspaper headlines screamed of 'chat wars' and unattributed insults flew between the two men. So-called 'friends' spoke of bitter rivalries and secret snubs, all of which may have helped the ratings but didn't make for a good atmosphere at Broadcasting House. And, after dismissing all the early stories as nonsense, Jonathan finally started to worry about how seriously others might be taking them. He decided the decent thing to do was to get in touch with his supposed tormentor.

'Dear Terry, I am writing to apologise for the tabloids...' was how he started the letter he wrote from his dressing room in 1991. Terry wrote back, saying no offence had been taken, and Jonathan, still surprisingly star-struck, says he kept the letter for years.

On a slightly less gallant note, however, Jonathan was prepared to speak out against his holiday-cover rival, Sue Lawley. She looked to have retained her status as Terry's first-choice replacement, even after Jonathan's well-received two-week stint. And he couldn't understand how that could be.

'OK, Sue is a better journalist than me but she doesn't have a sense of humour. The essence of a chat-show host is the ability to make people laugh. Sue is very good at probing into hard news stories but, as far as showbiz gossip goes, she just doesn't make the grade. I think I was better than her. The BBC should be looking for a cult figure to take off where Wogan should leave off. But I do not believe Sue Lawley is that person. People accuse her of being patronising and I don't think she's very good.'

It was a rare and uncharacteristic attack on a fellow professional. And showbusiness insiders say it reveals that, for all his bravado, Jonathan's confidence was still little more than skin deep.

Making matters worse was the fact that not everyone was pleased with Jonathan's temporary move to BBC1. Former fans were accusing him of selling out. And some said he would no longer be welcome back on the supposedly edgier Channel 4. Had he risked his lucrative niche position there for a couple of weeks in the spotlight on *Wogan*? Looking back, Jonathan says he was painfully aware of what American friends told him was 'tall-poppy syndrome' – that he had been built up only to be chopped down and that this chopping would manifest itself in a particularly British attack on both his motives and his credibility. 'There is a credibility thing in England. There seems to be an attitude that says to be credible, to be worth watching or listening to, you can't be mainstream or successful in a popular way or a financial way because that then renders what you are saying obsolete or invalid. I know I can be seen to be selling out – doing lots of dodgy ads and shows and things for the money. But I react against the accusations because I am doing something I love, as well as to pay the rent.'

The boy whose Leytonstone household saw all television stars as of equal validity, and said mass-market entertainment could be a window on a wonderful new world, couldn't see how being popular could automatically be seen as a bad thing. Jonathan just wanted to be himself, and do the things he loved. But he suddenly felt that this was starting to annoy people, and he started to worry how dangerous the backlash against him could be.

Fortunately, not everyone saw Jonathan's stint on *Wogan* as selling out. Channel 4 boss Michael Grade saw it as a very high-profile audition – which he felt Jonathan had passed with flying colours. If there were indeed chat wars going on, then Grade wanted one of the big guns on his channel. He had been planning a big new chat show for some time, and now he was convinced he had finally found the right man to host it.

The 450-seater Greenwood Theatre near London Bridge was booked as the venue for the new show, which would again pile on the pressure by having Jonathan's name in the American-style title. *Tonight with Jonathan Ross* was going out three times a week – and it was going pretty much head-to-head with *Wogan* from the start. The first show (aired at 6.30pm, compared to Terry's 7.00pm) came out on Bonfire Night in 1990 and, puns at the ready, Jonathan said he wanted it to go with a bang. And, if the last 'chat wars' between him and Terry Wogan had been a press invention, this time around it was deadly serious. He said Terry was clearly 'exhausted and overexposed' and that viewers were 'crying out for something different'.

In order to provide it, Jonathan demanded a roving microphone for his show so he could march off into the audience whenever he felt like it to get reaction from members of the public – sometimes having them ask his guests questions while he smirked in the background. And, back on the stage previously used for a range of shows from *Question Time* to *Jackanory*, Jonathan admitted that his show would always veer more closely towards the latter. 'The fact is, I am trivia-based and proud of it. My show is silly, knockabout stuff,' he said. But that didn't mean it was easy to do. 'It is actually more difficult to do an entertaining show than it is to interview a cabinet minister when there are only a certain number of obvious questions to ask. Interviewing someone like Sean Connery in a lively way means you have to have your wits about you. It is a skill and I am proud to have that skill,' he said, on the defensive, as critics accused him of being too superficial.

What made matters worse was the fact that Terry, at 22 years Jonathan's senior, seemed to be easily beating him in the ratings. 'We won't knock *Wogan* off his perch overnight but I hope that, when we finally persuade viewers to tune in to Channel 4, my show will prove more popular,' Jonathan said when his show launched in November.

Unfortunately, this wasn't to be. *Wogan* continued to attract mainstream audiences of around 7.5 million, both before and after his young pretender launched against him. *Tonight with Jonathan Ross* got an average of 1.6 million and, as the Gulf War at the start of the decade got more serious, Jonathan's ratings fell as low as just 400,000. 'Jonathan Ross's show hasn't had any effect at all on our audience and our viewing figures have been constant since it launched,' *Wogan*'s head of publicity Gaynor Danity said.

Michael Aspel, then fronting a Saturday-night chat show of his own, was equally unperturbed about the competition from Ross. 'Jonathan is very personable but he will always be a specialised item on TV. He won't appeal to the squarer viewers.'

Channel 4 executives privately admitted that, at 6.30pm, Jonathan's show was on too early to attract the younger home-from-work audience it required.

And what of Terry himself? He dismissed Jonathan in three well-chosen sentences. 'I don't regard Ross as a rival.

He was overhyped and the show didn't deliver. He was interviewing people we had done weeks before,' Terry said when Jonathan's first series came to a close, and question marks arose over the likelihood of a second one. To rub salt into the wounds, Terry simultaneously announced that, on his upcoming 1,000th show, he was flying to Cannes for an hour-long set-piece interview with Madonna, already the biggest female entertainment star in the world. The chat coup would give his already high ratings a new spike. Without radical action, Jonathan's show could be dead in the water – alongside his reputation.

Fortunately, Jonathan was able to reveal some good news the day Terry flew out to meet Madonna in the south of France. After months of negotiations, he announced that he had poached Terry's long-term producer Jane O'Brien. She had a priceless reputation for wooing Hollywood names to Britain for interviews. In her new role, she would head up a team of producers and researchers charged with sharpening up Jonathan's show. The next time Madonna wanted to talk, Jane was determined to ensure that she talked to Jonathan rather than to Terry. And, in the meantime, she would be putting the same message out to all her other entertainment contacts. It was a huge shot in the arm for Channel 4 and a new series of *Tonight with Jonathan Ross* was immediately announced for September.

Jonathan was over the moon. He was back in business and, anyway, even if his ratings didn't pick up, he had an even bigger challenge waiting in the wings. The network chiefs wanted to see if he could crack America.

5

American Dreams

Jonathan had fallen in love with America as a shy comic-loving boy on his east London bunk bed. The country and its cities always seemed shiny and new. There might be dark corners where the bad guys lurked, but there were shafts of bright futuristic light as well. It seemed to be an optimistic, passionate place where anything was possible and even the unhappiest and most unlikely child could end up a hero. Jonathan and all the Ross children were brought up to believe that, if you work hard enough, then almost any dreams can come true. Even in Leytonstone in the 1960s, they had the American dream.

When he started to become interested in films, Jonathan's fascination with America intensified. He liked the way the people talked and what they said. He liked the way they lived. If he had been blindfolded and taken to New York, LA, San Francisco or any other major

American city, he reckoned he would have recognised his surroundings the moment the blindfold was removed. Conversely, if he had been dumped in Liverpool, Manchester, Glasgow or any other big British city, he reckoned he would have been mystified and alienated by his surroundings.

Nearly two decades after first watching American films on the family's new colour television, could Jonathan really build a career on the other side of the Atlantic? His inability to say his 'r's, his flat east London accent and his obsession with UK popular culture all seemed to count against him. He was, he felt, the epitome of Englishness back then. And surely that wouldn't work in the biggest entertainment market in the world?

Amazingly enough, station bosses in the States thought that it would. They saw the cheeky young Brit as a bizarre amalgam of each of the then top-three US chat-show hosts. They said he offered some of the flashness of Arsenio Hall, the droll and dry humour of David Letterman, and the enthusiasm and openness of Oprah Winfrey. The more the executives discussed their plans with him, the more Jonathan came to believe in them. Yes, he was immersed in British popular culture, but he had always been equally obsessed with the American equivalent. His short series, *Americana*, had demonstrated just how in tune he was with the country, and he had loved every minute of making it. Jane had travelled with him and they had laughed late into the night in various mid-Western motel rooms at the absurdity of what they were seeing and doing. In one show, *Viva Elvis!*, Jonathan had travelled across the whole country seeking out eccentric Elvis impersonators, including one who treasured a surgically removed wart and a toenail clipping from the star. Jonathan also dropped in at the annual Elvis impersonator competition at Bad Bob's Vapors in Memphis, Tennessee, and belted out his own version of 'Teddy Bear' dressed in blue suede shoes with his hair slicked back in a Presley quiff.

Funnily enough, the way the show was received both in America and Britain gave Jonathan a sense of how the wind might be blowing. 'Woss's Weally Weird Pwesley Impwession' was how one British paper reported the show, saying it lacked humour, warmth or style. American executives, however, loved it. They said it sparkled; they loved its irreverence and naughtiness. And they wanted more of the man behind it.

Donald Taffner, the man who had turned Benny Hill into a huge American star a generation earlier and had since taken the equally British farce *Run for Your Wife* to Broadway, was determined to put a deal together for Jonathan. And it was going to be a pretty unique arrangement. The original idea was for Jonathan's existing show to be given a bit of a makeover, to be filmed in London as usual, and then beamed back to American and broadcast coast to coast in the States. 'This is broadcasting history,' Jonathan told the US papers when the deal was announced. 'I love American TV and I just hope they love me.'

What thrilled him the most was the chance to work in the same market as David Letterman, his long-term chat hero and the man whose show had given him all the best ideas for *The Last Resort*. The thought of competing for viewers with David was thrilling and terrifying in equal measure. But Jonathan had only just turned 30. He was full of energy, felt he was at the top of his game and had nothing to lose.

Sadly, things didn't go quite the way Donald and Jonathan had hoped. Jonathan flew out for a series of meetings and high-level schmoozing sessions with station chiefs from New York to Los Angeles. But, for a while at least, it looked as if the American chat-show market was already too crowded to let some crazy Brit have a shot at it. And the idea of filming a show in London didn't seem likely to attract too many viewers in Kansas. So, while the 'meet and greet' tour of the studios continued, Jonathan had to accept that his big leap had to be put on hold.

He did see two other big dreams come true on that trip, though. First, as a potential new American star, he was invited on to the iconic *The Tonight Show* with Johnny Carson where he could learn first-hand from the real master of the interview genre. Then he got the chance to film an Oscar special for British television, for which Channel 4 had rented him a Bel-Air mansion to use as a base for interviews with the likes of Demi Moore and Jamie Lee Curtis.

Back in Britain, Jonathan and Jane settled back into their old routines. The American dream seemed to be over and they started to focus again on new challenges at home, which was when Channel 4 boss Michael Grade called another big meeting. Grade had been a long-term supporter of Jonathan, and reckoned there was far more to him than just the cheeky chappie creation beloved of the tabloids. Like Donald Taffner before him, Grade felt Jonathan could be an international star – the first Brit since David Frost to have a talk-television career on both sides of the Atlantic. And, just like Taffner, Grade had a uniquely complicated way of achieving it.

So in early 1992, Jonathan and Jane flew back to New York for another bite at the American pie. The latest idea was for Jonathan's show to be filmed in Manhattan before being beamed back to Britain and then sold to as many American stations as would take it. From the start, the producers pulled out all the stops. The show was going to need a lot of star quality to shine in America and, for a while, money was no object.

Jonathan and his team took over the famous Ed Sullivan Theater on Broadway in Manhattan for the recordings – another dream come true for the boy from Leytonstone. The 400-seat theatre was steeped in the kind of entertainment history Jonathan loved. CBS had taken it over in 1936 and Ed Sullivan, the original king of vaudeville-style television variety shows, had filmed there for more than 20 years and had ultimately given it his name. Since 1993, it had also been where the *Late Show with David Letterman* was filmed. So, for Jonathan, it was hallowed turf indeed. It was where legends and heroes were made. And it seemed incredible, absolutely incredible, that he was now working there.

Equally impressive was the quality of his first few guests. Actress Kathleen Turner gave her first ever interview to a British chat-show host on Jonathan's show.

Cher, Jodie Foster, Michael J Fox and Brooke Shields all appeared as well. With many Americans unwilling to fly after the recent Gulf War, the idea of going to them, rather than expecting them to come to London, seemed to have paid off.

Unfortunately for Jonathan's big dreams, all the Hollywood stars and theatre magic in the world don't count for much in television if the ratings don't hold up. American stations didn't buy the show in anything like the numbers first hoped for. And back in Britain, Terry Wogan continued to rule the chat-show roost. Channel 4's American adventure looked an expensive mistake. So Jonathan was called home and reinstalled in his old south London Greenwood Theatre for another three-times-a-week series. But, even then, it looked as if he might not be safe. After six more months on air, the newspapers were full of rumours that this show was going to be cancelled as well. 'We continue to regard Jonathan as a major talent and we shall still be giving him a high profile,' a Channel 4 spokesman was quoted as saying in response. As votes of confidence go, this disturbingly vague comment was lukewarm at best. And so Jonathan decided he would jump before he was pushed.

Having spent so much time watching American television over the past few years, Jonathan's mind was buzzing with new show ideas and formats. He had installed a huge satellite dish outside his and Jane's new house in Chalk Farm, north London, so he could also dip into some of the best and (perhaps more interestingly) the worst television from other corners of the globe. Italian game shows, German documentaries, Japanese endurance ordeals – plus chat and variety shows from Poland, Belgium and France. Jonathan soaked them all up, watching and learning every day and long into every night.

With so many ideas in his head, Jonathan was soon ready to move on from his chat-show chair and try anything and everything new. And, despite the American failures, he was feeling more confident about his abilities than ever before.

'When I was first on television, I was just finding my way and working on instinct because everything was so new. Now I think I have a feel for what works and what doesn't, so I can be more focused,' he said. That was the good news. The bad news was that Jonathan's new confidence meant he risked taking his eye off the ball. That was certainly the case with his next high-profile show – the primetime *Saturday Zoo*. His career nightmare was about to begin. 'For the first time, I am doing a show that I want to watch, without worrying so much about what the viewers want to see,' Jonathan said just before the first recording began. With hindsight, that was his first big mistake.

When putting together the original *Saturday Zoo* pitch, Jonathan once again surrounded himself with several comedians and performers who had first appeared on *The Last Resort* and had since become close friends. Steve Coogan and Mark Thomas got early breaks on *Saturday Zoo*, and there were big roles for Jonathan's long-term sparring partner Rowland Rivron and Jilted John performer Graham Fellowes. American comedian and soon-to-be film star Denis Leary was brought over to perform, while Joanna Lumley was also on board as an occasional co-host. When working out who to have as the other guest stars, the planning process was simple, relaxed and great fun. 'Whoever we think is clever, amusing and funny, we say, "Great. Let's get them on," and we do,' said Jonathan. But, while this sounds easy, Jonathan admits that below the surface he was paddling away like crazy to ensure everything went smoothly when the guests arrived. 'The real success in what I do comes from the preparation I put in,' he said when asked about his achievements. 'Contrary to what some people assume, I do actually work very hard on the interviews, for hours and days beforehand. I read as much as possible. I write many questions then cut them down and restructure the interview, then I might put some gags in or some jokes. So, every interview I go into, I have personally put a lot of work into it. I have never gone into an interview and done it off the top of my head.'

That was important, because the overall guest list for the show was as stellar as anything Jonathan (or indeed Terry Wogan) had ever achieved on their chat shows. Throw in a mix of comedy, quizzes and songs and the show certainly didn't lack any fizz. Jonathan was even making his first foray into the acting world by taking part in some of the pre-recorded sketches and spoofs. But would the show win the ratings war, or had the world moved on from the Ed Sullivan days Jonathan had researched in New York? In an uncharacteristic moment of self-doubt, Jonathan admitted that he wasn't sure, but that he was damned if he wouldn't give it everything he had.

'In the beginning, I had a mild anxiety that I wasn't going to be able to do anything new or interesting with the guests... I worried about *Saturday Zoo* not being fresh,' he said with real self-awareness. 'I always know that I can deliver a basic level of professionalism but in a way that scares me more than anything else because that could mean that I might end up doing this job for ever. I'd rather fail spectacularly doing something interesting than carry on not doing anything new and everyone ignoring me. I've never felt I am on TV with some sort of God-given right. I feel I'm only there while I can come up with good ideas. And even if they don't work I hope people appreciate that at least I was trying to do something interesting.'

As it turned out, viewers and critics were not prepared to offer him this kindness. *Saturday Zoo*, launched with high hopes and all the best intentions, was widely dubbed an anachronism and a career-stopping disaster. Jonathan was shell-shocked about the savagery with which it was received. But, having had his face on so many screens and magazine covers for the past five years, Jonathan should have expected that the comments would finally start to get personal... which they very soon did.

'Pardon me, but I seem to have lost the point of Jonathan Ross,' veteran critic Jack Tinker wrote in the *Daily Mail*. 'Didn't he used to be the bloke who asked all the questions no one else dared? What happened while I wasn't looking? Did someone come along and clamp his curiosity? Did he undergo an IQ transplant? Or does he now only do it for the suits and the tax-free haircuts? But what exactly is it that he does, anyway? That is now the question.'

There was worse to come. 'Smiling a lot at what other people think is funny doesn't qualify on my Richter scale of entertainment,' continued Tinker. 'I sat in mounting bewilderment last weekend trying to discover any sign of recognisable human intellect at work on his behalf in his aptly named *Saturday Zoo*.'

The wild clothes were still there, other critics said. But it seemed as if the wardrobe mistress had 'sprayed them all over in some humour-resistant Teflon', as the *Independent* suggested. And, while Naomi Campbell's appearance on the first show of the series was followed by many other big-name guests, Jonathan was widely criticised for wasting the opportunities he had with them.

His big coup, and proof that he had grown hugely in stature since the early days of *The Last Resort* and *Tonight with Jonathan Ross*, was finally to win over Madonna for a guest slot. But the critics said he put in a woeful performance in the interview – which was subsequently listed as one of the worst of all time. 'Big John actually coaxed this shy, retiring debutante to discuss such life-enhancing matters as toe-sucking. Big deal. Try stopping Madonna from talking dirty. That's the real scoop,' Tinker concluded dismissively.

And, with *Saturday Zoo* killed off, it seemed that Jonathan had a lot more bad career choices, and bad reviews, ahead of him. In the summer of 1993, *Fascinating Facts* was yet another example of professional misjudgement. The basic idea might have been good – Jonathan presented the 13-episode ITV show with wild-eyed enthusiasm, investigating everything from phonecard swapping to secret recording devices. But the timing was way off. By the early 1990s, these sorts of shows had begun to look dated and clichéd. When he investigated trends from abroad, it was clear that almost everything he wanted us to laugh at had already been unearthed by the likes of Clive James and Chris Tarrant. As television genres went, this one had long since been colonised and exhausted. Television insiders said they couldn't understand why someone like Jonathan who had once been at the cutting edge could have agreed to do it. The segment on bent cucumbers – with a distinct whiff of 1970s *That's Life* – was particularly dire. Once more, the criticism was personal and it really started to look as if Jonathan's glory days might be over.

'Can Jonathan Ross ever shake off the reek of the eighties that clings to him like a particularly cloying aftershave? Not on the strength of *Fascinating Facts*,' concluded critic India Knight. 'Mr Ross, as host of the seminal, if derivative, *The Last Resort*, became famous for his perky sharp suits, perky Post-Modern sets and, above all, for his admirable and unprecedented directness during interviews. Well, these days, I don't know how he can face himself in the mornings. Jonathan Ross is highly talented. Why, then, is he grinning inanely, interviewing people about funny cucumbers and gastric noises? All the Thierry Mugler suits and kitsch sets in the world won't save him now.'

Jonathan, though, wasn't prepared to go down without a fight. No sooner had one show been savaged by the reviewers and taken off air, than he was back with another. The only problem was that each new show seemed as uninspiring as the last. *Gag Tag* is widely seen as another best-forgotten programme from the era. Jonathan shared top billing with old friend Frank Skinner but the reviews were harsh. 'Not original and just not funny,' was one of the most succinct. Audiences agreed and voted with their remotes by changing channels in their droves.

Other bad experiences were also leaving Jonathan feeling battle-scarred by his position as the supposed golden boy of British television. An anonymous caller rang Channel 4 and made a death threat against him while he was making a guest appearance on *The Word* with Terry Christian, for example. And, while crank callers are commonplace in the entertainment industry, the authorities took this one seriously enough for the station to call in some private security guards. The men watched over Jonathan 24 hours a day until the threat was thought to have passed.

They were sobering times indeed for a man who had joined the entertainment industry saying all he had ever wanted to do was have fun. And, as the pressure for a new hit show mounted, Jonathan found himself making some pretty spectacular misjudgements.

One of the men he had started work with back on *The Last Resort* was Vic Reeves. At that point, Vic had been just another researcher and hopeful gag writer. But he and his comedy partner Bob Mortimer had since ridden the stand-up wave and become mainstream successes with shows like *Vic Reeves' Big Night Out* and *At Home with Vic and Bob*. In 1993, they had another typically offbeat idea for a new show and wanted to see if Jonathan would

Jonathan in 1987.

Jonathan in the *Last Resort* days, the show that made his name.

Top: Actress, singer, but most notably ex-wife of Sylvester Stallone, Brigitte Nielsen was a guest on *The Last Resort* in 1987.

Bottom: An early awards connection – in Soho Square with students modelling designs from the student fashion awards in 1987.

Top left: Jonathan and Jane in 1991.

Top right: The young family Ross.

Bottom: All good friends, but Madonna would not always prove to be an easy interview for Jonathan.

Top: More cigars as Channel 4 boss Michael Grade poses with Jonathan.

Bottom: Showing some moves with Rowland Rivron (far right) who appeared on *The Last Resort* and Richard Branson, who gave Jonathan a radio job after hearing him on Radio 1.

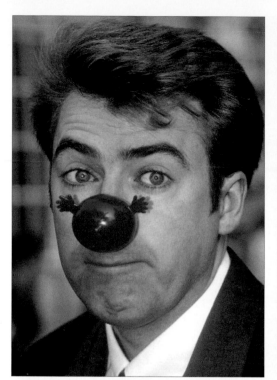

Friends in comedy and charity:

Top left: The 1991 year of Comedy Relief.

Top right: On stage with Jack Dee.

Bottom: At a party with Bob Geldof in 1991.

Top: Vic Reeves and Jonathan and youngsters in 1994.

Bottom: Jane and Jonathan enjoying the Irish-flavoured music festival Fleadh, in London's Finsbury Park.

Top: Film fan Jonathan Ross gets to hang out with one of the greats, James Bond's Q, Desmond Llewelyn.

Bottom: Presenting an award with Melinda Messenger at the 1997 MOBO (Music of Black Origin) Awards.

come on board with them. The show was to be called *Shooting Stars*. It was a comic panel-based quiz show where questions would focus on the showbusiness world and be interrupted by an endless stream of skits and in-jokes. Jonathan agreed to film a pilot show and turned up at the central London studio to be a team captain opposite old pal Danny Baker. Also on board as team members were Martin Clunes, Noddy Holder and Wendy Richard and everyone says it was a fun, if anarchic experience. But would the show really work as a series? Jonathan and Danny both had their doubts, so, when the BBC finally gave the show the green light, they both turned down the chance to come back as full-time team captains. Ulrika Jonsson and Mark Lamarr got the big breaks as replacements, while an unknown 18-year-old comedian called Matt Lucas was also taken on board to read out the 'scores on the doors'.

As everyone now knows, *Shooting Stars* turned out to be one of the biggest television hits of the decade – making stars out of everyone from Matt Lucas upwards. Jonathan did come back for a single episode later in that first stormingly successful series. But, as the regular stars made show after show and headed out on a massively lucrative national tour, it looked as if turning down a regular role on *Shooting Stars* was going to go down as one of Jonathan's biggest and most expensive mistakes.

But, in a similar vein, and amidst similar company, Jonathan had other career humiliations to endure before regaining his poise. *Never Mind the Buzzcocks* was another cult success with a huge mainstream audience, again on BBC2. But Jonathan's on-screen involvement was hardly going to boost his confidence. Over the years, he made four appearances as a guest panellist and, in his first, he started to speak only to have host Mark Lamarr tell him to 'Shut the fuck up'. In just those four words, it was clear how far Jonathan seemed to be falling. What wasn't clear was whether his career could ever recover.

6

Showbusiness

Thousands of fans who had loved Jonathan's irreverent, wildly dressed style since those first Channel 4 shows back in 1987 were struggling to understand what had happened to the presenter over the ensuing decade. The confusion and sense of betrayal came to a head when he followed up his latest flop with a couple of tacky, low-rent commercials – including the infamous Pizza Hut example in which the whole focus was on Caprice making fun of his speech impediment.

'People came up to me in the street back then and said, "Why are you doing this?" and my first thought was, "What the hell has it got to do with you?" But then I thought it was actually really sweet of people to care. And I had to accept that they had a point,' he said afterwards.

And, while Jonathan continued to pretend that everything in his life was going well, the truth was that pressure had been building up behind the scenes since

1987 – pressure that was soon about to come to a head and explode.

Jonathan's problem was that he was never just the presenter on any of his programmes. When he and fellow researcher Alan Marke had first had the idea for *The Last Resort*, they had been advised to set up their own production company to produce and market it. And so, after weeks trying to come up with a suitable name, Generation X had been born. Running a media company, like running any other firm, is not as easy as it looks, however. And, unlike his on-off friend Chris Evans, Jonathan didn't take to it at all. Finding lawyers, accountants, auditors, staff and even premises felt like a waste of time when all he and Alan wanted to do was offer a single show to Channel 4. So, at first, Jonathan only gave that side of the job a minor part of his attention. But, by the time the first adrenalin-fuelled series of *The Last Resort* had ended, the company was demanding ever more of its founders' time. They no longer saw it as a vehicle to get their one show on air. It could be a way to produce countless other shows as well – some for Jonathan, some for the other stars-in-the-making that they were beginning to count as friends.

Vic Reeves was one of their first proper employees – and he scouted out several other key talents while turning himself and Bob Mortimer into fully fledged stars. Meanwhile, comedian Sean Hughes and future *Little Britain* stars Matt Lucas and David Walliams were also getting involved one way or another. All of them would get an early lift up the entertainment ladder with

Jonathan's help – and Generation X's output threatened to spiral out of control. At the end of 1989, for example, they put a huge amount of time, effort and money behind a potential Rowland Rivron vehicle called *Go with Scrote*. Based on their favourite childhood show *Go with Noakes*, the new six-part show was based around the surgically inept character of Dr Martin Scrote that Rowland had first aired on *The Last Resort*. In the end, the show disappeared without a trace. But that didn't seem to matter. Back then, Jonathan's simple love of being in the television industry meant he was prepared to do whatever it took to push his company forward – he would ignore any temporary setbacks and failures and move swiftly on to the next project when required. 'I have never worked with anyone who puts in more hours,' said Alan as another series of *The Last Resort* was commissioned. 'His only problem is that he wants to do everything himself. But everybody likes working with him because he inspires people. He's extremely sharp at picking up trash culture ideas. Television is very disposable, it has no shelf-life, so you have to react to things quickly, which Jonathan does.'

Or at least he did, until his management role became too much to bear. Media company accountant Peter Swettenham says running a successful production company means juggling a whole series of balls and that delegation is vitally important. 'If you have never been in business before, or have only ever been an employee yourself, you don't realise just how much admin there is to running a company. And, in the entertainment industry, the size of the budgets involved and the number of payments you are constantly making can be eye-watering. If you don't have a head for business, you can get blinded by all that and lose your focus on what you really want to do.'

And, outside of Generation X, Jonathan was also finding it hard to cope with some of the new decisions he was being forced to make. Being in demand and having his talents recognised was wonderful. But the man who had gone in front of the cameras because he thought it would be a bit of a laugh was suddenly aware that comedy becomes an extremely serious business when you get to the top of the tree. Having seen how successful he had been on Channel 4, the BBC and ITV were both keen to give him exclusive deals of their own. The great news was that they were both offering telephone-number-sized salaries to try and woo him. The bad news was that every offer seemed to be accompanied by contracts the size of telephone directories. It was all getting too much for the lad who just wanted to fool around and make some documentaries about his favourite film directors.

Part of Jonathan's problems back then stemmed from the fact that he kept all his insecurities and worries under wraps. Aware that he was being paid huge amounts of money and effectively living his dream, he knew it would be churlish to moan about the pressure. So he carried on, trying to please everyone and do just about everything.

Generation X had moved into cramped but stylish offices just off Wardour Street in London's super-cool Soho and staff who worked with Jonathan back then say that he was always one of their favourite bosses. He remembered birthdays, sent flowers when secretaries were off sick, was happy to muck in with everything from photocopying to tea rounds and never missed leaving parties or other corporate bonding sessions. Behind closed doors, though, only Jonathan knew how thinly he was spreading himself. And, as Generation X grew and grew, Jonathan suddenly realised that something had to give.

'I suddenly realised I was depressed, very depressed – even though I had never felt like that before and hope I never will be again. I couldn't sleep. I lay awake for hours every night worrying about the future and dreading the next day. I was very tense and confused, never cheerful like I usually am and it ultimately put a strain on everyone and everything.'

But still the most unlikely documents were placed on his desk requiring his urgent attention – he had to make decisions on insurance, health and safety legislation, tax and VAT, staff pensions... It was all taking him further and further from what he loved most – the chance to be creative in front of the cameras. He started to feel stifled and a vicious circle ensued. Worried about the original documents he had signed when setting up the company, he started to worry about the new ones he and his staff were signing now. If there had been problems back then, then surely there could be new problems now? Jonathan was finally ready to admit he was struggling.

'I had found myself in a position of great responsibility in a successful company with no business knowledge. I had signed a contract which bound me for years and I hated the fact that I didn't have any freedom. To keep the company going, we were trying to keep me in production as much as possible and my shows were suffering as a result. There wasn't time for me to take a breather and think about what worked and what didn't, and about what, exactly, I wanted to do.'

Other industry insiders agreed that Generation X was making strategic mistakes by taking the easy option and pushing Jonathan in front of every camera it could find. 'They need to get away from a reliance on a single star and develop a stable of talent. They have to do other things,' said Berrand Moulier of the independent television producer's association Pact. But, for every offshoot programme with Vic, Bob or one of the other stars in front of the camera, there still seemed to be several ideas focused squarely on Jonathan. His cheeky grin and quick jokes were the cornerstone of the company. But, as *Gag Tag* and *Fascinating Facts* viewers could no doubt see, they were becoming increasingly forced.

For all his reservations, Generation X seemed suddenly to have turned into a corporate juggernaut. Neither Jonathan nor anyone else could stop it now. On the cards at his lowest point was a massive co-production deal with the mighty HBO channel in America – where, as you might imagine, for the most litigious capital on earth, the legal documents alone were overwhelming. Jonathan was the world's biggest fan of American television and some of the best HBO shows. But the shows themselves didn't seem to be what this deal was about. It was all about money, positioning, brand awareness and the other issues that he couldn't care less about. So the whole co-production deal, which seemed to take forever to set up and ultimately ended up going almost nowhere, sapped Jonathan's spirits even further.

The perfectionist in Jonathan also found himself hating the conveyor-belt style of programming he seemed to be involved in. An unlikely result of his early success was that no one seemed to have the guts to say 'no' to him any more. And that, in itself, depressed him and stifled his creativity. 'I felt I could go to Channel 4 and offer them almost anything and they would take it. I was becoming complacent, coasting along and directionless.'

As the pressure mounted, Jonathan found himself thinking back to the fight, the excitement and the challenge of the early days when he and Alan had been unknown researchers with big dreams. Being outsiders trying to break into and fight the system had been a lot more fun than lying back in the fat, corporate reality they now inhabited. And that fat, corporate world was about to make even bigger demands of them.

Television was changing dramatically in the early 1990s, and Jonathan and Alan were being urged to think really big to take advantage of it. Mike Bolland, the Channel 4 commissioning editor who had given Jonathan and Alan their first big break, was now Generation X's managing director, and he was putting together a massive bid for the new Channel 5 franchise. If it went ahead, it meant taking on some big-time partners, including soon-to-be Italian premier Silvio Berlusconi's media group and, unlikely as it seems, Strathclyde Regional Council. It was complicated high-stakes stuff, and Jonathan hated having to try and get his head around it. Perhaps the final straw for Jonathan, as that deal also came to nothing, was the fact that he could no longer rely on some of the people he was supposed to delegate work to. The company had got too big, recruitment had perhaps happened too fast and Jonathan feared it was all his fault. He started to get paranoid and angry, which made everything even worse.

'I had created this company but it was all going wrong for me. I was going into an office every day and sitting there with people I didn't really respect who were earning money off me. I had invested seven years of my life in that company and was watching it flounder because people there weren't up to speed. It was heartbreaking. But people had contracts and I found it very hard to confront people in those days.'

Back at home with Jane, he tried to clear his head. For months now, Jane had been telling him he had to wrest back control of his life. But, after trusting her advice implicitly since the day they had met, he says he unaccountably started to ignore it. 'She had always been right in the past so I don't know why I stopped listening when things got really tough,' he says.

When he started listening to her again, he agreed that only drastic action would save him. 'I thought, "What am I doing with my life? This is complete and utter junk," and I was so fed up of coming to the office every day for endless meetings about fatuous projects that were never going to happen. It had been building up inside me like a pressure cooker until, one weekend, I just exploded and said, "That's it. I'm getting out. I'm walking away." And I did.'

The production company, which at that point had an

annual turnover of between £3–4 million, had an estimated £750,000 in the bank. As its joint-founder and the star of all its most successful shows, Jonathan should have been able to claim a huge percentage of all that, as well as a share of any future earnings from his shows and formats. But he realised that to get this would have involved even more meetings with lawyers, more documents, more arguments, more stress. And he didn't want to know. He walked away, signing away all claims to the company in return for a final one-off payment of... precisely £1.

The television industry reeled when the news was announced. Jonathan had been seen as a media mogul in the making; he was the backbone of Generation X. And two key questions began to be asked from the Groucho Club to Broadcasting House. Would the company survive without him? And, more importantly, would he survive without it?

Jonathan says the latter was never far from his own mind. 'It was very scary because I had a big overdraft and no other shows lined up. That Christmas, I felt very, very stressed over money, which I had never really felt before and hoped I would never do again. I realised I owed a fortune and I felt I had let Jane and the family down because I never wanted us to be in that kind of situation.'

Unfortunately for everyone, Jonathan was on the edge of a broader downward spiral. He was hugely relieved to be out of the corporate jungle. But the relief was tempered with fear that he had no new world to make his own. He grew his hair long, stopped exercising and started comfort eating – junk food, huge snacks in front of the television, sweets and chocolate in bed. Within a couple of months of leaving the company, his weight topped 15 stone and, looking in the mirror one day, he says he caught a whiff of Michael Winner. It was not a good feeling for a 30-something former cover-boy and lad-about-town. 'I spent a lot of time in bed, just going "Uh-oh" because I think you just retreat into the womb when things go wrong,' he says. 'It was very hard to move forward at that time, to go to meetings and project a confidence I didn't feel.' And that confidence wasn't helped by the newspapers – one of which got a particularly unflattering photograph of him heading out of a bar one evening. It seemed as if Jonathan was having a very public mid-life crisis. And he was only 34 years old.

More disturbingly, the work simply dried up. The rising star of British broadcasting, the man who had exploded on to our television screens and turned the industry upside down, was branded yet another burned-out television has-been. Producers and network executives stopped taking his calls; new ideas he had were politely ignored; and a new generation of presenters, often in his image, were taking his place in front of the cameras.

At one point, it seemed as if the only job on offer was as host of the bizarre so-called family game show where the losing family's granny was to be hoisted ever further off the ground by a crane. What was worse was that Jonathan came close to accepting it.

What was bothering him the most was a nagging feeling that he had been naive – wrong about the whole broadcasting industry. 'It is hard to be taken off the air in Britain. I've made some good shows and some bad shows, but they just let you keep on making them,' he told one of his American heroes, David Letterman, when he was invited on to the star's eponymous show in the early 1990s. Nearly half a decade later, and having effectively taken himself off the air, Jonathan was finding it disturbingly difficult to get back on. 'When I started out, my vanity was such that I couldn't possibly conceive of a time when British TV could wobble along without me,' he said. Learning that, far from wobbling along, it could race ahead at dizzying speed was a sobering thought.

What Jonathan wouldn't know until later was just how close he had also come to extreme personal and professional embarrassment at this terrible and stressful time. Something else had happened which could have squeezed out what little life there was left in his career – and only the kindness of a most unlikely friend was to save him.

The unexpected crisis had arisen out of the way Jonathan and Jane had decided to tackle their increasingly busy schedules. Feeling that they sometimes only saw each other in passing when one handed over the childcare duties to the other before dashing out to a work meeting, they had taken to communicating occasionally by computer. That turned out to be a mistake – as the editor of the *News of the World* was to be among the first to find out.

Piers Morgan says a member of the public got in touch with the paper one day in early 1994 saying he had found Jonathan Ross's laptop and was willing to sell it to them for what seemed like a ridiculously high sum of £20,000. 'When we asked the guy trying to flog it why on earth it was worth so much, he leered and said, "Because there's so much filth on it,"' Piers wrote in his private diaries – since published as the bestselling *The Insider*. 'We had a look to see what he was on about and, sure enough, there was an extraordinary 2,000-word missive from Jonathan to his wife Jane which could best be described as "graphic", detailing precisely what he'd like to get up to with his young bride.'

What could have been damaging, as well as embarrassing, for Jonathan was that the laptop also contained all his contact numbers, business accounts and scripts for several new shows. In the wrong hands, this kind of material could have triggered professional as well as personal disaster. But Piers was ready to offer the right hands.

'Jonathan's a kind of mate and I want to hire him as our new movie critic,' he wrote in 1994. 'So it was his lucky day that this guy came to us, claiming implausibly to have "found the laptop in a taxi".'

The *News of the World* paid the seller a knock-down £3,000 and got on the phone to Jonathan. He could get the laptop and all its information back – but only if he played ball while the paper had a bit of fun with him.

A mortified Jonathan – whose first thought on realising that his marital fantasies might be in the public domain was for what his mother and mother-in-law might think – was ready to play whatever game Piers required. Piers said he was going to run the story about the 'love byte' letters without quoting directly from them. And he wanted Jonathan to go on record confirming them. This Jonathan decided to do with typical aplomb. 'It is embarrassing in this day and age to be exposed as an out-and-out heterosexual who still wants to have sex of the filthy variety with his wife, but there we go. I plead guilty,' he told several million *News of the World* readers.

What Jonathan couldn't know, until perhaps he read *The Insider* more than a decade later, were the editor's final thoughts on the matter. 'Not sure that I'll ever be able to look at him in quite the same way,' Piers wrote of his prospective columnist. 'I wonder if he knows a load of my staff have read the letter? Probably. He's quite media savvy.'

With so much going wrong in his life back in 1994, Jonathan should have rejoiced when he was suddenly offered an amazing golden escape route. He might have left Generation X with just £1 and no lucrative rights to his former shows but, after nearly a year in the entertainment wilderness, the BBC decided to offer him a huge new contract. They had wanted to poach him for years and felt the time was right to bring him into the mainstream. Sign the contract and Jonathan knew his career would have been back on track and all the family's finances would have been straightened out overnight.

But Jonathan refused – because he had just decided to follow an entirely different path. 'I don't know if it was brave or stupid not to sign that contract when I didn't know what else there might be around. We lived in a huge house in a nice position but, if it had meant moving away from there and adapting my lifestyle, I was prepared to do that. I realised it was more important that I respected myself and enjoyed what I was doing and could therefore be more supportive to my family,' he said.

Family was suddenly going to come first for Jonathan. Against all expectations, he was prepared to stay out of the entertainment world for a little longer. He wanted to stay at home and watch his children grow up.

7

Family Man

Having met and married so quickly, it was no surprise to their family and friends that Jane and Jonathan decided to start a family as quickly as they could.

'Before we met, it had never been in either of our game plans to be parents so young, but after we were together it just seemed the most natural step in the world. We were ready for it,' says Jane. She got pregnant when she was 20 and Jonathan was 29 and the couple's first baby, the 9lb 12oz Betty Kitten Ross, was born 12 days late in July 1991. Jonathan was at the St John's and St Elizabeth's Hospital in north-west London for the birth – a long, tough labour that had left Jane utterly exhausted.

Back at home, Jane thrived on being a mother. But Jonathan, constantly busy at the time with *Tonight with Jonathan Ross* and all the behind-the-scenes machinations at Generation X, was not yet ready to be the perfect father. 'I still wanted to be out with my friends. I assumed that if I wanted to do something then off I could go and do it,' he said. It seemed that you needed to be very strong to keep your family together in the entertainment industry, and Jonathan admits that, while he could see the problem, he had not yet found the strength to deal with it. 'In television, it is easy to lose touch with your real life. You're being flattered all day long and you go home feeling very self-important. I wasn't yet ready to see how much I needed to change my life now I had a family.'

What Jonathan did know was that he needed to keep working and keep earning, because, when Jane had first got pregnant, the couple had decided to upgrade from the pink three-storey house they had owned in north London's relatively modest Chalk Farm for the past three years. That summer, they had found what they were convinced would be the family home of their dreams. It was less than a mile further north, but could just as well have been in another world. Built right on the edge of Hampstead Heath, it had fantastic views out over the countryside and some celebrity neighbours to die for. The Ross family also had plenty of friends in nearby streets – from Boy George to Frank Skinner and David Baddiel – and they could all meet up a short walk from the Ross front door in the bars and coffee shops of Hampstead Village. What made the new house even better was its size. It had five bedrooms spread over four floors so there would be plenty of room for baby Betty and any other children who might come along.

There were two problems, however. The first was the price tag – a hefty £350,000, which, back then, was a staggering five times the average UK price. The next potential problem was that, even at this price, the house wasn't ready to move in to. A huge amount of work needed to be done to bring it up to scratch, which would swallow up even more cash. So should they risk everything and buy it?

After nights of agonising, the couple decided that they would. Their offer was accepted, surveyors and builders took a look and, within weeks, the whole property was covered in scaffolding. Six months, £100,000 and a huge amount of stress later, the trio moved in – just in time for Christmas. Two new bathrooms had been added, and the house now had his and hers offices, a nursery and a games room. 'It's the best house in England and I don't think we will ever want to leave it,' Jonathan said as the removal vans began unpacking.

On the downside, it brought with it some of the country's largest mortgage payments as well – interest rates had just soared to more than 11 per cent and the economy was reeling. As the couple had decided to keep on their old house rather than sell it, they needed to pay out more than £5,000 a month to their banks. That is still a huge amount of money today. But it was particularly bad back then when the Halifax says the national average mortgage repayment, even at the sky-high interest rates of the day, came in at well under £500 a month.

Desperate to tough things out, the Ross family were clearly in the big league. And, as Jane tried to become pregnant again, they both started putting in the hours to ensure they could stay there. Jane's big idea was a series of self-help books for teenagers – a gap in the market she had spotted back in her days on *Just Seventeen*, what felt like a lifetime ago. In 1993, after the couple's second child Harvey Kirby Ross was born, she was ready to make it a reality. She started on the research, met up with agents, publishers and publicists and produced *Thirteensomething – A Survivor's Guide.* Her idea had been to produce a light-hearted, accessible and realistic guide for young teenagers on everything from school, dating, parents and eating disorders. What she deliberately didn't cover was smoking, drinking, drugs or sex. 'I feel that, if teenagers are already smoking, drinking or doing drugs, they won't want to hear advice on it anyway and, if they're not, then they don't particularly want to read about people who do. In the case of sex, it is a huge subject that you can't cover briefly as you would have to in a book like this.'

So, with the first book out of the way, Jane started work on a second, which would tackle the tougher issues. 'I still think it is important to be both light-hearted but sensible. A lot of articles about sex in teenage magazines are 90 per cent about safe sex, which is obviously the most important thing but which does leave a lot of questions unanswered that need answering.'

In the end, Jane wrote four advice books for teenagers – and, by the time the final one was about to be published, she had become a mother of three. Jonathan, Betty, Harvey and Jane's mother Amanda had all been back at the St John's and St Elizabeth's Hospital in February 1997 when Honey Kinny was born – weighing in at a hefty 8lb 14oz. 'I felt very connected to that hospital as our other children had been born there and I liked the idea of having the same birth team,' says Jane. 'This time, it was a natural birth and Betty and Harvey were there to see her come out and they were absolutely delighted. I'm sure that's why there's been virtually no jealousy from either of them. Having my mother there as well meant it turned into a really lovely family day.'

After the press had asked for and got their first pictures of the latest Ross arrival, the couple could no longer run from accusations that they had out-Geldofed the Geldofs when it came to their children's bizarre names. Jonathan refused to accept it. 'I think our kids' names are great. Their first names – Betty, Harvey and Honey – all seem perfectly normal to me.' And he said that none of the less orthodox second names had been picked at random. All meant something – with varying degrees of seriousness. Harvey's middle name was a homage to Jack Kirby, the comic-book artist that both his parents loved. Honey's was in honour of Jane's childhood nanny – the same 70-something lady who had looked after her mother and who got a connection to a third generation of the Goldman family in the naming process. And Betty's middle name? Well, both parents thought she looked a little like a kitten when she was born.

What also set the Rosses apart from many of the other rich neighbours in Hampstead was the fact that they were still refusing to take on any full-time staff to help them. Jane, in particular, wasn't keen on the thought of farming the children out to nannies or childminders. So her mother came over to help look after the children one day a week while Jonathan's mother helped out on another. Kinny, her longstanding family nanny and now a dear friend, was also on hand for emergencies. 'I'm intensely lucky to have all this,' Jane admitted at the time, saying she needed two full days a week to focus on her advice books. And, as it turned out, someone else was waiting in the wings preparing to take on an even bigger slice of the childcare arrangements – Jonathan.

His wake-up call as a parent had come in several forms. The problems at Generation X were about to reach their peak; he was increasingly unhappy with the prevailing wisdom in the broadcasting industry that you're a nobody if you are not on television. And then there was something else. His eldest brother Paul was suffering from yet another throat illness and newspaper headlines screamed out about his latest 'cancer scare'. Visiting Paul at his home after one of the 13 operations he had over the course of three tough years, Jonathan started to feel the first hints of his own mortality. And, as he and Jane pitched in with the rest of the Ross family to help look after Paul and Kerry's three children, he got a sense of his true role as a parent as well. Paul was never suffering from a life-threatening illness as the newspapers had suggested. But if life could be taken away at any time, then how do you really want to be remembered? As a television star? Or as dad?

Jonathan realised he wanted to pick the latter – just as a second medical emergency forced him to do just that.

A couple of years earlier, when he had been filming some shows for the music channel VH1, he had spent two months living in a flat in LA with Jane and two-year-old Betty. Jane, heavily pregnant with Harvey, had been largely housebound and had become obsessed with American television. One night, she and Jonathan watched the first episode of a new television show in their apartment. It was called *The X-Files* and both were convinced from that first evening that it would be a hit.

Jane was also fascinated by the true stories which might lie behind the plotlines and, back in London, she made some calls to see if there could be a book in it. It turned out that there was, indeed, a book to be written – and a bestselling one at that. *The X-Files: Book of the Unexplained* was first published in 1995 and sold more than 400,000 copies in hardback, cementing Jane's new reputation as a profitable author. The research reawakened her interest in psychic and other phenomena and a whole new career was about to be born, culminating, years later, with her own series of television shows on the subject.

For a while, though, it looked as if the first in the two volumes of *X-Files* books would never get produced, because, just after Jane had signed a contract to write the first of them in four months, she suddenly came down with what appeared to be a severe fever. She was sweating, her body and her legs ached and she felt a strain in her side whenever she tried to get out of bed. After nearly a week of the same symptoms, she went to the doctor to be told she had a severe gall bladder infection, and was hospitalised while her body fought to recover from the attack on her system. Jonathan called in the cavalry in the form of his and her relatives, and led the relief effort to ensure that Jane could recuperate and work in peace when she came home.

'Jonathan is Mr Mum – getting the children up, taking care of them, doing everything,' Jane said at the time. 'The book deadline meant working 16-hour days, at weekends, and skipping meals. I'm not complaining because I enjoyed it, but I only saw the children for an hour or so before their bedtime and that broke my heart.'

Jonathan's 'new man' home life didn't end, though, when the manuscript was submitted and Jane was back to full health. 'Working and having children is a juggling act for everyone and what is nice for us is that Jonathan sees it as a juggling act for him as well,' says Jane. 'I think he's unique... the best dad in the world.'

What Jonathan felt was that he was the happiest dad in the world as well. Being forced to be a full-time parent, just after the low days of his post-Generation X depression, had given him a new enthusiasm for life.

'All I wanted to do was make shows and spend the money on my family. I wanted to go and play with the kids and have some time with them. So that's what I started to do. I hated spending all my time in meetings about business. My view was: what's the point of having loads of money just so you can go to work to earn more money? I don't understand that. My main wish is that our kids have a nice childhood. I wouldn't have them feel I wasn't there. Work isn't as important as having a good time and being with my family.'

Of course, Jonathan being Jonathan, heartfelt comments and sentiments like this couldn't be allowed to stand without a more light-hearted follow-up. And when he was asked to advise others about becoming a parent, he was happy to let rip. 'When you have a baby, the little stranger that has been introduced into your life will be just that. A little stranger,' he told a caller to his radio show years later. 'You will never understand what is going on in its irritating little head. It will cause you nothing but heartache and pain and, let's not forget, huge expense. All those little things that you treated yourself to in the past? Not any more. Little weekends away on EasyJet? Not any more.'

Have children and, for the next 18 years, everything, Jonathan says, will be based around 'the mewling, red-faced monster... the tyrant that will sit on your shoulders like a supernatural beast'.

And, when he is on the subject, Jonathan is happy to provide some typically forthright parenting advice, not least on the subject of teaching children about the reality of the world they have been born into. 'Kids need to know it is not all plain sailing. You've got to teach kids that life can be unfair,' he advises. And he reckons you can do that by occasionally modifying the end of their bedtime stories. 'And then the muppet babies all died and went to hell...' being one of his favourite conclusions. 'And then they were all run over by a bus... Sleep tight,' being another. 'You don't end every story that way. But, when you do, it's a more useful message, preparing them for the knocks that life has in store for them.' The Ross children have yet to comment.

On a more serious level, Jonathan was increasingly starting to think about the future in the mid-1990s. He decided to do more exercise so he wouldn't one day be the fattest and oldest-looking dad at sports day – he was also determined that, having spent so much time and money building up his unique wardrobe, he wasn't suddenly going to be too fat to fit into any of his clothes. He also had a new level of priorities in his life. Since becoming a more involved father, he decided family must always come first. Friends would come second, and business would be last on his list.

As an example, when Betty was six, Jonathan looked in his diary and saw he was due to take her and Harvey to a Sooty show at the weekend, support his friend Frank Skinner by being in the audience for his new show on the Monday, and go to the première of the new Bond film *Tomorrow Never Dies* on the Tuesday. Sooty and Frank were both allocated quality Ross time, but James Bond had to save the world without him – Jonathan cancelled his première invitation at the last moment and stayed at home instead. 'I just didn't feel I could go out again,' he said the next day. 'My family need me more than anyone else. You shouldn't go out every night if you're a parent. If you want to go out all the time, don't have kids. It's that simple.'

Funnily enough, it was at *The Sooty Show* that Jonathan realised that his children did subconsciously appreciate what he had started to do for them. 'Matthew Corbett asked them what their dad did for a living, and they said, "He works in the kitchen." I was officially a house husband and I actually thought that was a pretty good thing to be.'

Jane tells a similar story from when Jonathan had been hosting a television awards show in the mid-1990s. It had been a rare night out for the two of them, as she had been in the audience to watch her husband perform. 'When

Harvey saw Jonathan on TV, he told our babysitter that Daddy was going to come out of the set in a minute to fix him what he called a milky bot-bot because that was the kind of thing Jonathan always did. Harvey wasn't even two at the time and hadn't quite grasped how Daddy got into the telly in the first place, but I know that, if Jonathan could figure out a way to magically fly out of the TV and back into our living room, milky bot-bot in hand, then he would do so.'

Another sign that Jonathan had taken a huge career back seat came when the family flew to Vancouver in Canada when Jane was on a tour to promote the first *X-Files* book. 'The hotel was booked in Jane's name and I found myself being addressed as Mr Goldman. I was dismayed,' he jokes – though, off the record, he admits he was actually very proud.

As the children got older, Jonathan says he started to enjoy their company even more. 'With Jonathan, even watching a video becomes a special treat for the kids, with popcorn, jam sandwiches and hot chocolate, a cosy nest of cushions and blankets to snuggle into and all the lights turned off. When the children's friends come over to play, they never want to go home,' says Jane. And, despite his famous love of B-movies, horror and martial arts films, his children have turned Jonathan into a softie on the entertainment front. 'One of his all-time favourite films is *Toy Story*, and I am sure he won't mind me saying that he always cries at the end when the little boy is reunited with his cowboy and spaceman dollies,' says Jane.

For his part, Jonathan says he is a lot tougher in other

departments – including discipline and good behaviour. 'We are obsessive about the children saying "please" and "thank you" and not being noisy in public,' he says. 'Teaching children to have respect for other people is incredibly important. We don't want to produce spoiled brats that no one likes.'

Jonathan says one trick to keeping the whole family happy is multi-tasking and lateral thinking. So, on Saturdays, when the kids were young and the weekly shop needed to be done, he would take all three to their local Safeway and either put them in the crèche or have fun pushing them round in a trolley while he got the groceries. Jane, meanwhile, was at home working and happy in the knowledge that the kids were having fun while the cupboards were restocked. Jonathan taught all three of the kids to swim in their local council pool and, until recently, went swimming with them there every Sunday morning. The man obsessed with his own clothes was also happy to do the children's laundry a lot of the time in the hope that they would look as good as their dad. He admits, though, that accidents with ketchup and ice cream normally made sure this wasn't going to happen.

Looking back, Jonathan and Jane say these early years as a family were fantastic for all of them. Jane's books were bringing in plenty of money, while Jonathan's awards gigs and occasional game-show guest appearances also helped keep the family finances in the black. But, however happy he was at home, Jonathan was starting to pay a lot more attention to the world of work. And it seemed that the industry – and viewers – really did miss him. The *Independent*'s television expert Michael Collins was one of the first to point this out as, one after another, the young pretenders to Jonathan's former light-entertainment crown fell by the wayside. It seemed as if being a successful show host was not as easy as it sometimes looked.

'The television front-man who can dovetail a show, think on his feet and be funny is fast becoming an endangered species. Sadly, one of the last of this dying breed, Jonathan Ross, is barely seen on the box any more,' Michael commented.

It was a sentiment that an increasing number of other people seemed to share. 'This is no criticism of you, but you don't seem to have made the most of your career,' Chris Evans told his friend in the low days after Generation X. It was turning out to be the understatement of the year.

Chris, whom Jonathan had first met while doing a radio show, was turning out to be the older man's mentor and inspiration in a surprising number of ways. Neither man was exactly known for being diplomatic or holding back from saying what he thought. So there was little surprise that the media wanted to portray them as at loggerheads with each other and suggested they were the best of enemies rather than the closest of friends. But Jonathan was always ready to cool things down by acknowledging his supposed rival's strengths. If Chris wanted to be called the new king of cool TV, then that was fine, Jonathan felt. And the ginger dynamo was certainly welcome to the title of Britain's biggest media mogul. 'Someone said to me recently, "Chris is a bit like you were six years ago," and I said, "No, he's far more successful than I ever was." And that's true. He's also a much better businessman than I will ever be.'

Chris also turned out to be a more generous friend than many people had expected. In the mid-1990s, when Jonathan was playing happy families and staying semi-detached from the television industry, Chris asked him to be the host of a new show – *TFI Friday* – that he was planning to produce. The original idea was to have a primetime grown-up slot on ITV and Jonathan says he was incredibly tempted to break his self-imposed purdah and agree to it. But, in the end, he pulled out when ITV decided not to take up the option and Chris signed an alternative teatime deal with Channel 4. 'It was always going to be a fun show but I just didn't want to do the new version. I felt I was too old to sit around interviewing 17-year-old pop stars and pretending that I cared about them.'

But, while the show went ahead without Jonathan and made an even bigger star of Chris, the planning process behind it had reawakened Jonathan's love of ground-breaking television. 'When Chris and I started working on the early idea of *TFI Friday*, it made me realise that there was still a lot of fun to be had in television. I got the bug again.'

In his years out of the limelight, Jonathan had already decided there was a Newtonian law that could be applied to the entertainment world. 'It's celebrity physics. That which is hot must grow cold. But that which is cold can be reheated, if you're careful enough.'

At 35 years old, Jonathan was finally ready to get back into the kitchen.

8

The Comeback Kid

If you are going to make a comeback, you might as well make a big one. That was Jonathan's view in 1996 when he signed his first major deal since leaving Generation X. And, in the late 1990s, you didn't get much bigger than London Weekend Television. The station was based next to the National Theatre on the south bank of the Thames in central London and sold its programmes to the whole of the ITV network. Once inside the high-rise head-quarters, every corridor seemed lined with larger-than-life photographs of some of the huge stars who had made the company such a success. Cilla Black, Dame Edna Everage, Judi Dench, Michael Aspel, Michael Barrymore, David Frost... from comedy to drama, news programmes to kids' shows, LWT had dominated popular culture for some 30 years.

Having his own big, brightly coloured photo put up amidst such illustrious company was an enormous thrill for Jonathan. Especially because a tiny voice inside him

117

was worried that he had somehow passed his own sell-by date. 'At 35, I realised my fame had outstripped my achievements and I knew that I had to change. I also knew I was no longer the fresh little darling of TV. When I first came along with *The Last Resort*, I was different to everyone else. But now you have Clive Anderson, Ruby Wax and all the others doing the same sort of thing.'

Would Jonathan have a new unique selling point with which to woo viewers? And just what sort of shows did LWT have in mind for him?

Nigel Lythgoe, the station's controller of entertainment, was first in line to reassure his new signing publicly. 'Jonathan Ross is a great name and he has been out of it for a little while. It will be good to see him back on screen because he has a lot of talent,' Nigel said, as the two-year deal was announced.

The plan was for a mixture of one-off and regular shows – and, from the start, the film buff in Jonathan was in seventh heaven. His first big task was to research, write and record three main shows – *In Search of James Bond*, *In Search of Tarzan* and *In Search of Dracula*. And, with the LWT brand behind him, Jonathan had access to everyone he had spent a lifetime wanting to meet. So for James Bond he got interviews and contributions from the likes of Sean Connery, George Lazenby, Roger Moore, Timothy Dalton and Pierce Brosnan – as well as comments from Bond villains played by everyone from Honor Blackman to Robbie Coltrane. He even spoke to some real-life secret agents to get their take on their fictional presentation. The shows were a typical mix of childlike irreverence and genuine respect, as well as some barely disguised lechery when he got to interview Bo Derek for the Tarzan show.

Having been out of the game for what felt like years, Jonathan was over the moon to be back among such exalted company straight away. And there was more to come, because, as well as meeting Chris Eubank and Nigel Benn for the *Best of Enemies* interview, he was going to try his hand at yet another chat show, *The Late Jonathan Ross*. In the end, this only lasted a single series, but it served its purpose by reminding everyone who Jonathan was and why he had been so popular first time around. And it helped prepare audiences for his first ever Saturday-night outing.

This show, *The Big Big Talent Show*, was billed as a cooler, younger version of *Opportunity Knocks*. The 'clapometer' and 'send in your favourite's name on a postcard, please' style of voting on Hughie Green's old show was to be replaced by a slightly more high-tech studio audience and telephone vote with Jonathan. But because no one had yet thought to film the auditions rather than just the selected performers, *The Big Big Talent Show* was never quite going to have the edge of a *Pop Idol* or an *X-Factor*.

Looking back, Jonathan admits that his own fascinations with the offbeat, the bizarre and the downright weird may have stopped the show from being as successful as the Simon Cowell-style versions of the following decade. From the start, Jonathan fought against having the contestants dominated by straight-haired female singers and teenage boy-band wannabes. So the six performers who did get their breaks each week were certainly an eclectic bunch. Alongside the singers came magicians, ventriloquists, comedians and dancers. Each was introduced by a friend or relative, who sat with Jonathan and explained why their act deserved a showcase on national television – the notable exception here being one of the favourites of the second series, comedian Ed Byrne, who was unaccountably introduced by his bank manager.

After the performances, the *Sun*'s Garry Bushell was on hand to give a Cowell-style critique of them before the studio and then phone votes began. The whole of the first series was filmed live, in front of more than 500 people in LWT's biggest underground studio. That alone made the experience worthwhile for Jonathan. 'I think the only way forward for me now is to work in front of a really big live audience and I can't wait,' he said as the first show approached.

Unfortunately, by the time ventriloquist Paul Zurdin was announced as the winner of the first series in 1996, the gloss was already starting to come off the show for Jonathan. The station had decided that the next series would be recorded rather than broadcast live, which seemed too safe an option. And Jonathan says the pressure to have ballad-singers dominating the performance list was starting to get him down. That said, the show was still capable of springing a few surprises. Another big find was Iranian stand-up comedian Omid Djalili, who has since broken into Hollywood with roles in everything from *The World is Not Enough* and *The Mummy* to *Casanova*. And then, of course, came Charlotte Church.

Charlotte's cabaret-singing aunt, Caroline Cooper, was the one who had been picked to perform on Jonathan's show – and she says the whole family had to beg Jonathan and the producers to allow her to be introduced by 11-year-old Charlotte. 'They said they usually wouldn't let children go on in case they got tongue-tied,' says Caroline. But, even at 11, there was little danger of that with Charlotte. As part of her brief chat with Jonathan while Caroline's cabaret band got ready, Charlotte admitted that she, too, was a singer. Up for a bit of fun, as ever, Jonathan challenged her to prove it – while the cameras rolled. So the tiny 11-year-old stood up, took a deep breath and sang the first four lines from Andrew Lloyd-Webber's 'Pie Jesu'. 'The whole studio froze. No one could believe that such a huge voice could come out of such a tiny body. Everyone forgot all about me,' Caroline joked afterwards.

Jonathan admits that he also felt a real star had been born on his show that night. 'It crackled, the atmosphere was incredible. To say the hairs stood up on the back of your neck is an understatement. You just knew this girl had something special,' he says.

Though back then, of course, he had no idea just how successful she would be – or that the four lines of music that she sang on his show would effectively win Charlotte her first £100,000 five-album deal and catapult her into the entertainment elite.

Some people felt that Charlotte's unscripted introduction of true star power was somehow part of the reason that the rest of the series fell flat – no one else could really generate the same frisson of excitement in the studio.

After having had such high hopes for the variety-show genre, Jonathan was turning out to have second thoughts about it. His role on television had always been to shake up old formats, to introduce viewers to something new. But even he couldn't seem to do that to a poor man's *Opportunity Knocks*. 'It was a successful show but perhaps I shouldn't have been doing it,' he said when the dust had settled on the second series.

Critics agreed. 'Ventriloquist Paul Zurdin won the 1996 series; a 16-year-old singer Lydia Griffiths won in 1997, and the viewers won in 1998 when the show failed to return for a new series,' was how The Custard Television website put it in its list of the top-ten 'best-forgotten' television talent shows.

Not that it had been all bad, however. The money Jonathan had made on the LWT contract helped him realise a dream – buying a bolt-hole for the family in America. He and Jane both loved the hot sun, the wild rains and the stormy, muggy nights of Florida, so, after a series of reconnaissance trips, they picked a house overlooking a private beach some 150 miles north of Miami. It wasn't particularly grand, by American standards. But with three storeys, a vast family room and huge marble en-suite bathrooms, even adjoining the children's bedrooms, it was a far cry from the crowded house of Jonathan's own east London childhood. The one thing the house didn't have when the family bought it was a pool – so they got the designers and diggers round and had one built. The design they picked had wide, sweeping curves, a shallow hot-tub area and featured a long-tailed gecko in tiny ceramic tiles on the blue floor.

Over the years, the Florida home would be both the family's refuge and the place where Jonathan and Jane recharged and rebuilt themselves after the stresses and excesses of London. The couple also toured local thrift shops for unusual home decorations, just as they did in Britain. With their favourite kitsch almost everywhere, it wasn't hard to find the unique pieces they loved. Their bedroom, for example, was stuffed with Polynesian totem poles, bamboo screens... and a surfboard. In the early years of ownership, before multi-channel television arrived in Britain, the house was also where telly-obsessive Jonathan revelled in the chance to watch 160 or more versions of nothing 24 hours a day. Sometimes he would try to justify his telly watching by saying he was researching new show ideas for Britain. But mostly he was happy to say he simply enjoyed watching as much junk as the broadcasters could beam at him.

Back in Britain, after getting the keys to the Florida home, Jonathan did have another new venture on the cards, which was set to rejuvenate his spirits. Channel 4 was celebrating its 15th anniversary in 1997 and it planned to mark the occasion with some new versions of its most successful shows. *The Last Resort* was deemed to be one of them.

Jonathan pulled together a surprising number of his former colleagues – including some he had fallen out with over the Generation X debacle – to make a one-off episode of the show. Despite some early tensions, everyone got on well and had a ball when the recording date arrived. The big guests included Tim Roth, Helen Mirren and Quentin Tarantino. Frank Skinner did an Elvis number; an American lady promised to pop her eyeballs out; a man banged nails into his body. 'Ah, it's just like old times,' Jonathan cooed, trademark grin breaking out on his slightly rounder face.

But, for all the fun, everybody knew that *The Last Resort* couldn't do more than one show. It had shaken up the eighties, but the world had moved on and it was never going to thrive in the late nineties. Too much else had changed; too many other shows and presenters had parked their guns on Jonathan's turf. And, anyway, Jonathan himself felt the time had come for another subtle change of gear. 'From now on, I want to be very careful to do shows that I feel are right for me,' he said. 'I've been doing TV for a lot of years now and I would like to have a little dignity in my old age. The problem with the industry is that you do tend to get locked into a state of arrested adolescence, where you are allowed to carry on as goofily as you wish to be. It is only when you step back a bit that you think, "Hold it. Real people with real jobs don't behave this way." I don't mind doing the occasional silly thing but it is nice to act my age now.'

So totally anarchic variety shows were out. Jonathan was very aware that he was now a married man with children; he had grown up. From now on, he vowed that his work would have to reflect that.

Of all people, it was Chris Evans who finally gave

Jonathan the route map which would see him turn his whole career around and become one of the country's most loved broadcasters. And Chris did it by reminding him how much fun you can have on radio.

The ginger teenager, who had produced Jonathan's first proper show on the radio in 1988, had gone through a lot of ups and downs of his own since then, with many more still to come. The ups had included becoming an extraordinarily wealthy media mogul – one who had bought out Virgin Radio from Richard Branson and relaunched it under his Ginger Media Group umbrella.

Almost exactly a decade after they had first met, Chris wanted to work with Jonathan again. He was convinced that Jonathan's brand and banter were what Virgin needed – and so the Sunday morning gig, *The Jonathan Ross Show*, was born. The idea was for a typically lively mix of music, jokes, sketches, chat and general mayhem. Jonathan thrived on it – and on the endless leg-pulling that went on between himself and his boss. 'We're asking people which is their least favourite part of Jonathan Ross's show on Sunday or whether, like us, it's all of it,' Chris said on his own breakfast show one morning, as the fake battle got under way.

Jonathan fought back by suggesting that listeners wanted him to replace Chris on the daily show – but that he had to disappoint them. 'I'm not competing with Chris. I couldn't get up that early and do a breakfast show. Anyway, I'm much funnier than him. With me, you get a mature adult. With him, you get all this childish stuff. I mean, he's secretly 12. I've seen his body and he hasn't even reached puberty. That's why he's such an overachiever in every other area.'

As the barbs flew, the ratings rose, and Jonathan was having fun again. He had a great team of producers around him who largely selected the music he would play. 'You should see my own record collection. It is all music from Italian horror films. I'm not allowed to play anything I own,' he admitted in yet another self-deprecating spat with Chris.

More embarrassing for Jonathan (and for Jane and both sets of their parents) was another exchange Jonathan had in his radio studio one day. The day's show had been running for more than an hour when Jonathan accidentally left his microphone on while a record played (or when one of the production staff left it on deliberately; no one has ever been clear about exactly how it happened). What we do know is that Jonathan decided the time was right for a detailed description of what he and Jane had been up to the previous night. The mike only clicked off when things grew excessively pornographic and the station's phone lines had fired up with listeners wanting to complain or, perhaps unsurprisingly, to hear even more without what they thought was an annoying soundtrack in the background.

Incidents like this aside, the show was another great training ground for Jonathan and, as usual, he was always ready to improve his skills.

'How do you think we did today?' Jonathan tended to head to the lobby of the Virgin Radio building for a coffee and a post-mortem with his producers after each weekly show. They say he was always happy for feedback and suggestions – though direct criticism was best avoided. It was there that a new friendship and a vitally important professional relationship were born. It was with a producer called Andy Davies, of whom Radio Two listeners would soon be hearing a lot more.

Buoyed up by the success of his new radio show and still loving being free of the corporate world, Jonathan couldn't believe how well things had turned out for him. Quitting Generation X could have left him almost penniless. But, nearly six years later, he seemed to be earning as much as ever. And he had plenty of time to enjoy it. 'The way I work now, I can take my kids to school every day and pick them up most afternoons. I work about five hours a day. I make a load of money and I am very aware that my kids won't be this age forever. Why do I need all the other hassle? I don't want to build an empire like Chris Evans. With an empire, you don't have time to fool around, to relax.'

With an empire, you also don't have time to go clothes shopping, he might have added. And that's something at which he and Jane were both becoming very good. 'We are a clothes couple,' Jane admits. 'But we accept that no one else seems to like our stuff. Maybe it's because we don't really like designer clothes. We're not Posh and Becks and I don't think either of us would set foot in Versace. We both get most of our stuff from the high street or in surf shops while on holiday. And, when we go out, it's not a deliberate competition to wear the most outlandish outfit. It's never for attention. It's just a matter of our taste. We just like funny, unusual clothes. Perhaps it is because we both grew up reading so many comics.'

One of Jane's favourite American stores is the cheap and cheerful Contempo Casuals – though she freely admits she is far too old to be shopping there. It aims itself squarely at 15–23-year-old women whom it asks to be 'stylisers', keeping their ear to the ground to pass on information about the latest trends and promoting the goods to other young people. Despite being more than twice the age of the store's key customers, Jonathan says he is inordinately proud that his wife has the confidence and the *chutzpah* to drag him and the kids into the stores and carry armfuls of clothes to the checkout.

For his part, Jonathan is equally happy to look like what he calls 'a surfer's grandfather' as he rifles through the hangers in American boarding stores looking for kit to wear at home. And the clothes he wears on screen or on big nights out? Jonathan's fashion sense – or possible lack of it – has always grabbed attention. One commentator said that it looked as if his wardrobe had taken the full force of an explosion at a car boot sale jointly run by Cher and Jackie Collins... with some aftershocks from one of Elton John's birthday parties thrown in as collateral damage.

And Jonathan is happy to own up to all his worst sartorial mistakes. 'The Gaultier shirt with elasticated sides? Loved it. But it made me look like an accordion,' he admitted. Having nominated his entire wardrobe for disposal when he went on Paul Merton's *Room 101* show, Jonathan also faced the music over his moment of madness going to a film première in a skirt – though he swore it was actually a kilt. 'It was the worst. Jane lent me her opaque tights, but stretched over my long legs they looked a bit sheer. Instead of a style statement, I looked like I had dragged up. For all the criticism he got, I thought David Beckham looked great in his sarong. I looked like the bigger blokes did when they did drag scenes in *It Ain't Half Hot, Mum*. A great big nancy boy.'

And, as the years went by, and his bank balance built up, Jonathan had been able to buy more and more clothes – both formal and informal. At one point, he estimated he had at least 60 designer suits, some in outlandish colours and designs perfect for television, some surprisingly sober for more private family occasions. But 60, he decided, had to be the limit. For years, he had been giving several away each year to friends and colleagues. And, as the new millennium approached, he started to auction some for charity as well. But, even then, he couldn't resist a joke at his own expense. 'I share the same tailor as David Beckham,' he said proudly when promoting one sale. 'But you'll see that they have to make my trousers with an elasticated waistband.'

The only problem Jonathan found when he first started to auction his clothes off for charity was that he could buy even more in exactly the same way. It turned out that Cherie Blair was not the only big name who looked for second-hand shoes and clothes on eBay. Jonathan says he has been a big online buyer of 'vintage Vivienne Westwood bondage shorts and gay naked cowboy T-shirts' ever since he first logged on to the site. Bad enough, you might think. 'But what's worse is that he sometimes wears them on the school run,' Jane says ruefully. And she's not joking.

'When I drop the kids at school looking scruffy and wearing quite ludicrous and wholly inappropriate clothing for a man of my age, the parents go, "Oh my God!"' Jonathan admits. 'But one term, when I was working more during the day and doing the afternoon run straight from a meeting, one of the mothers said, "I must say, you're dressing much smarter this year." Unfortunately for her, it didn't last.'

To his credit, Jonathan was never going to change what he wore on screen just to please his critics in the media. He didn't dress the way he did because he wanted to shock or to get noticed. He picked his clothes because he liked them. The boy who had spent his childhood wearing hand-me-downs from his shorter elder brothers loved the freedom of finally being able to choose his own clothes. He loved the fact that he dared to wear what so many other men wouldn't even touch. For one big awards show, the *Sunday Telegraph* once predicted that he would wear 'one of the kind of cod-couture abominations that he genuinely, and rather touchingly, believes he looks good in'. And the paper was right. Jonathan did think he looked good in some of his most extreme colours and clothes. They made him happy and they didn't harm anyone else. So what was so wrong with that?

Fortunately for Jonathan, his wife was never prepared to join in the chorus of disapproval his outfits often triggered. 'Jane is wonderful,' he says. 'She lets me wear ridiculous flared trousers and Jean-Paul Gaultier kilts to movie premières without getting embarrassed and has never, ever, said I look too old or too fat to wear some outrageous new fashion. Pretty much as long as I don't wear anything that actually lights up or requires batteries, then Jane will let it go.'

And it is not just on the issue of clothes that Jane gives blanket approval to her husband's whims. She had been just as keen to find kitsch furniture and furnishings for their first house (where the fake leopardskin curtains had been the focal point of the dining room). More unusually, perhaps, when Jonathan was 34, and at that point a dad of two, Jane had applauded when he had his belly button pierced. 'There is no logical or acceptable mature answer,' he said when asked why he did it. But he was childishly pleased with the result – lifting up his shirt and showing off the piercing to Pierce Brosnan in LA during an interview about the latest James Bond film. 'Pierce laughed like a drain. And in a good way. I am sure I detected a note of envy,' Jonathan claimed afterwards.

Not to be outdone, Jane decided to get a couple of piercings of her own. The first, a silver stud, went in the crown of her left ear. The second was somewhere a whole lot more personal. 'Only Jonathan gets to see that one, of course,' she says discreetly. 'But it's not a fetish thing in any way. When I got it done, I actually wanted to get my eyebrow pierced but I do have to do the school run and there are limits.'

For Jonathan, this was a classic example of the way his wife mixed rebellion and responsibility. And he loved her for it. He had always loved the fact that Jane was prepared to look as unconventional as he did – and in the late 1990s he says he quite literally gave her a round of applause when she walked into the room one evening having gone from her natural state as a brunette to something a little more, well, traffic-stopping. She and a friend had bleached out her old colour and applied a dye they had found called Poppy Red – as well as some near-permanent hair extensions. Job done, and traffic did pretty much start stopping, especially when she and the family went on holiday in the deeply conservative communities of coastal Florida. 'To say heads turned out there is an understatement,' he says proudly, accepting that the pink lizard tattooed on his wife's right thigh and her love of big, pearly, stick-on nails and garish rings may also be contributing to the effect.

At just under 6ft 2in, Jonathan towers over Jane's 5ft 6in when they are out together, but when they are snapped walking into a restaurant or at a film première, he says it is always obvious that they are made for each other. Calling her 'glamorous, voluptuous, exotic and unique', he buys almost as many clothes for her as he does for himself – from second-hand hats to Vivienne Westwood corsets.

The latter, of course, accentuate Jane's extraordinary figure. 'I confess to becoming famous for my cleavage,' she says smiling. But she admits that this wasn't always her defining feature. 'I was a really late developer as a teenager. I was tiny, quite skinny and then I generally exploded all over so it was hard to tell if I had big boobs or not. When I got pregnant with Betty at 20, some of the boobs stayed afterwards so I ended up having a second growth spurt. Since then, by and large, I've always been very happy with having large boobs,' she says.

And she has always seemed happy showing them off. 'I think it is great to celebrate your best features,' she says of some of her more up-front outfits, admitting that, after years assuming she was a 34DD, she was, in fact, a 32F. 'If I had amazing legs, I would walk around with short skirts. But I don't look good in high-neck tops. I look like I'm smuggling something and it comes over a bit matronly so I need to go for low necks.'

Her gravity-defying personal style has also unfairly pegged Jonathan as a boob man, she says. 'But I wasn't like this when we first met. I guess they have developed along with our relationship. I like my shape and it is nice to know that Jonathan really likes it, too, even though it wasn't what he originally went for.'

For his part, Jonathan says it doesn't matter for a second what he originally went for – winning thousands of female fans in the process. 'Jane gets no pressure over weight from me. I love her fat... I love her thin. When she was pregnant, she looked fantastic, too. She is my ideal, whatever she is.'

Unlike many men, Jonathan is also prepared to describe his own battles with his weight. Over the years, he has gone from a low of around 12st 8lb to a high of nearly 16st. But his reactions to the changes are not always what you might expect. 'I sometimes enjoy looking a bit overweight on television,' he says half seriously. 'It means I'm not being employed just because I was a pretty young thing from the eighties. It's pleasing, in a perverse kind of way, to feel I can look worse and worse and still be working. Though I admit that the way the television industry is set up, it seems to be only men who can get away with this.'

That said, over the years, Jonathan has found himself empathising with the way high-profile women are sometimes attacked by the media for their looks – because papers often treat him in exactly the same way. As part of a preview to the Brit Awards in 1996, he dressed up as everyone from David Bowie and the Beatles to a punk rocker, for example. The *Daily Mail*, in particular, was not impressed by his Bowie. 'It is a brave attempt. But Jonathan Ross is a little on the large side to pass for the Thin White Duke. The elaborate silver make-up – worn as a tribute to David Bowie, whose music was instrumental in helping to shape the seventies – cannot begin to conceal Ross's portly torso or chunky arms. He ends up looking more like a scary monster than the svelte rock star's flamboyant persona of Aladdin Sane,' it wrote under the headline: 'POP ORIGINAL ROSS TRIES NOT TO POP OUT OF HIS COSTUME'.

Unashamedly vain and surprisingly sensitive to criticism, Jonathan could only just see the joke. And he made a mental note to stop that sort of thing ever being said again. He happily shares Jane's on-off obsession with diets and can sometimes be childishly pleased with the results. 'The only time in my life when I have ever been really fit was in my late thirties and it was quite remarkable. For a very brief period, I could actually see my stomach muscles. It was quite alarming and, to be honest, I didn't always feel very comfortable because that is not how I see myself. I felt a bit awkward, strange even, when I used to catch a reflection of myself. Which, obviously, I made sure I could do as often as possible every day, taking a longer route coming downstairs at home so I could go past the one big mirror and so on. It was nice briefly having almost a *GQ*-type figure because clothes do look better. But it was never going to last.'

What would last was his and Jane's ability to make an entrance. When they were invited to old friend Boy George's 40th birthday party, the invitation stipulated a 'dandies and courtesans' dress code in tribute to the New Romantics fashion of Culture Club's glory years. Jonathan and Jane were in seventh heaven. Jane decided on a black basque, split skirt and fishnet tights. Jonathan, meanwhile, had decided to out-George the birthday Boy. He had picked a feathered fuchsia-pink hat, a glittering gold lamé suit, frilly shirt and a full face of make-up. The photographers went wild – and, in the next day's papers, other well-dressed guests like Barbara Windsor, Kylie Minogue and Tracey Emin were all but ignored.

Worryingly, though, if anyone thinks the couple look wild on their big nights out at parties, film premières or awards ceremonies, they should consider what they wear on quiet nights in. 'Jonathan's got a Spiderman outfit and a lovely black Elvis jumpsuit which he has worn a lot,' says Jane. 'We once had an Elvis dinner party where we served up deep-fried peanut butter sandwiches and Jonathan wore his catsuit. Best night ever.'

9

Ross on Film

As 1998 drew to a close, Jonathan and Jane were both on good form and both acting entirely in character. Jane had bought a new car – after years of zipping around town in a powder-blue Hillman Imp, she had bought one of just 20 Nissan Figaros to be imported to the country, and the only one that was finished in lime-green with shiny white leather seats. And why did she choose that kind of car over the more conventional Porsche, BMW or Mercedes that her earnings could have afforded? 'Because it's so cute. It's the kind of car that makes people smile at you and wave, rather than frown and cut you up,' she said simply.

Jonathan, meanwhile, was talking to friends about having a tattoo done in time for the following year's Valentine's Day – he ultimately decided to have Jane's name written on his right arm in scrabble letters (for, despite their image as a cutting-edge cool showbiz couple, the pair say they look forward to long games of Scrabble when their children are sleeping).

What neither Jonathan nor Jane knew as they got ready for yet another family Christmas in their Florida home was that both their lives were about to change dramatically. They were in for some huge professional highs and some terrible personal lows. Coping with both was going to put a huge amount of pressure on their marriage. The final year of the millennium, 1999, was one both were looking forward to, but it would turn out to be the one they would soon desperately want to forget.

Jonathan's high hopes for the New Year had been raised some six months earlier when he heard the rumour that Barry Norman was considering giving up his longstanding job as the BBC's resident film critic. Barry had been presenting his show for a staggering 26 years – the latest incarnation was *Film '98*, which ended its run in July. Most of those years had been very successful and Barry had won just about every broadcasting award, spoken about every film and interviewed every major figure in the industry. But, as the nineties came to a close, it was an open secret in the broadcasting world that Barry, then 64, was unhappy about the time slots the BBC was giving his show and the promotional effort it was putting behind it. Equally well known was the fact that several rival channels were wooing him with lucrative contracts if he ever decided to jump ship.

So could the biggest film-based job in television finally be up for grabs? As the rumours started to abound, Jonathan found himself in a surprisingly sensitive position. Unknown to most people outside of the entertainment set, his younger sister Lisa was married to one of Barry Norman's nephews – so Jonathan had family connections to tap and possible inside information to gather. But did he want to win the biggest job of his life and have the triumph tarnished by accusations of nepotism? And wouldn't it be a bit tacky, anyway, to get his little sister to push his case with her new family?

In the end, Jonathan knew he had to sit back and try to win the role on his own merits. He called his agent as the rumours of Barry's departure finally became public knowledge and said he would do anything to go up for the role. And, just as he did so, the news was confirmed. Barry was off to Sky, where general manager of broadcasting Elizabeth Murdoch called him 'the face and voice of film in Britain' and said his new shows would be required viewing for every film fan in the country.

Jonathan immediately found himself in a crowded field of hopeful presenters, all vying to star in a show which some said might even be axed. For much of the summer, there were rumours that *Film '98* would be the last of the franchise because the BBC didn't think there was any future for a mainstream review programme. Then Jonathan took a call from his agent. *Film '99* was indeed on the cards, and the BBC wanted Jonathan to film a pilot episode to see if he should host it. The show was produced in secret in a tiny studio in Broadcasting House. Jonathan tried to project the right mix of enthusiasm, knowledge, credibility and humour. And then he went home to wait for news.

What worried him as he did so were the identities of the two key presenters he was competing with. Both were younger than him – a worry as the BBC had specifically said it wanted 'someone who could appeal to a younger audience' to replace the 60-something Barry Norman. More importantly, both had impeccable film credentials. The husky-voiced Mariella Frostrup was the first of them, and her CV in many ways was a mirror image of Jonathan's. She, too, had presented acclaimed documentaries on James Bond; she had presented video review shows and, for several years, ITV's flagship cinema show *The Little Picture Show*. She picked up the cool youth vote with appearances on everything from *Shooting Stars* to *Have I Got News for You* and she could win the worthy older vote with her broadsheet-newspaper experience and her Radio Four arts shows. She was also sexy and female – which were the two things even Jonathan couldn't compete with... though he swore he would dig out his kilt to try to swing the vote if he had to.

Next up, the rumour mill had it, was the 33-year-old former *Big Breakfast* presenter Johnny Vaughan. He, too, got the cool youth vote. And his Channel 4 *Moviewatch* show had gone down well with the critics too. In *Moviewatch*, Johnny sat with a panel of filmgoers who discussed the latest new releases. It had been a big departure from traditional film reviewing, and the BBC were said to be desperate for something new.

So did that push Johnny above Jonathan in the *Film '99* running order? And what about all the other rumoured rivals such as Gail Porter and Mark Kermode?

One extra worry for Jonathan at this point was the fact that he had just made his second attempt at film stardom – and the film in question was hardly one that was likely to ever appear on BBC1. The film was called *Pervirella*, and the eponymous central character was described as 'just your everyday sex demon with incredible lethal powers in her bountiful bosom'. And things became even more bizarre when the plot went under the microscope. For reasons far too convoluted to explain, *Pervirella* was to embark on what one reviewer described as 'an incredible adventure that takes her to every continent and exposes her to incredible dangers – her only weapon being her incredible lust'.

And this was only one element of the thrills on offer to audiences: 'Delight at the scores of jiggling breasts. Gawp at the aboriginal gang-bang of death. Scream at the massive, masturbating man-tackle monster. Stare at the no-holes-barred lesbian romps. Gasp at the depraved bondage and fetish orgies of the evil cult,' the review continued.

Jonathan's role in the romp had come about through his well-known love of cult films and filmmakers. *Pervirella*'s director was Alex Chandon, who had made a name for himself in the pastiche B-movie world in the early 1990s with his super-low-budget film *Bad Karma*. He explains how Jonathan got on board in *Pervirella*. 'My mate's girlfriend was Jonathan's missus's best friend and gave her a copy of *Bad Karma* for a Christmas present. Apparently, they loved it. A year later, I was working for Channel 4, got talking to Jonathan and he confirmed it. I sent him my next film, *Drillbit*, asked if he would be in one of my films and he said "yes". Next thing I know, he and Mark Lamarr came along to be in *Pervirella*.'

Jonathan and Mark both had a ball during the brief manic burst of low-budget filming. Jonathan wore a long, golden blond wig under his rich red bishop's mitre of a hat – and had a blast. He pulled out his gold card at one bar to buy beers for the entire cast and crew after the day's shooting was over and made several new friends. 'Jonathan and Mark were both excellent and friendly and nice. But I think they hate the film,' Alex said afterwards – though neither Jonathan nor Mark has ever talked about it since.

To be fair to everyone involved, the whole film was made with its tongue firmly in its cheek. As Kenny Everett might have said, it was all done in the best possible taste. But, as it followed on from Jonathan's first cinematic venture, the spoof film *Raw Sex*, which he had made with Rowland Rivron and Jools Holland about 'a band that never existed', he was worried that BBC governors might decide he lacked the Barry Norman gravitas and was therefore unsuited to replace him and bring film reviews to the masses.

Fortunately for Jonathan, though unluckily for Alex Chandon, *Pervirella* hadn't exactly set the box office alight on its release. So Jonathan hoped it might have slipped under the BBC radar and wouldn't count against him.

As it turned out, Christmas had nearly arrived before anyone was to find out what the BBC was planning for the following year. Jonathan was sitting in his office at home when he took the call. After months of meetings and discussions, the BBC had made its decision – he was their choice to fill Barry Norman's shoes. *Film '99* would be back on air in the spring with Jonathan Ross in charge. Hardly able to believe it, Jonathan left his office at the back of the house – with views over the bins – and rushed up to Jane's, where the views opened out over Hampstead Heath. They hugged, and laughed, and got on the phone to family and friends with the news.

It was 22 December and it was the best Christmas present either of them could have imagined. 'When my school friends were dreaming about being Sylvester Stallone or Michael Caine, I wanted to be Barry Norman,' Jonathan says. 'I can hardly believe that I've finally made it. I'm a very, very happy puppy because it doesn't get any better than this for me. Going to see movies, then writing and talking about them and then being paid for it is just such a delightful prospect. How wonderful to know that a large part of my working week next year will be sitting on my backside watching the movies.'

With hindsight, perhaps, Jonathan shouldn't have been so flippant, because not everyone agreed with the BBC's decision and he found he still had some work to do persuading people he was the right choice. One contributor to the journalists' trade paper *Press Gazette* wrote that Jonathan got the job 'simply because he is a household name – an entertainer'.

'His experience of film reviewing is limited to a column he used to write for a Sunday tabloid,' another commentator said sniffily.

But both views were unfair, to say the least. As a mini-backlash started to build up, several powerful voices came out in Jonathan's support. Film was his forte, they said, and his passion. 'His enthusiasm is infectious,' said Andrea Wonfor, who was Arts and Entertainment Controller of Channel 4 when she gave Jonathan one of his early breaks and spotted how keen he was on the film world and all its players. She was convinced he was perfect for the BBC hot seat. 'I have seen him behave like an overexcited schoolboy before interviewing a personality who really interests him. And that can only help an interview, particularly as he has such an encyclopaedic knowledge of the industry.'

Jonathan himself was ready to fight back against the people who said he was too lightweight to replace Barry Norman. He repeated his belief that one of the best shows he has ever made was a documentary on the entirely obscure Finnish film director Aki Kaurismäki back in 1990. 'We had to fly all the way to the Arctic circle to talk to him and we stayed in a little village right by a lake so we were freezing cold and got stung by some kind of incredibly nasty insects. I had to sleep in a tiny child's bed in the same room as a man with the loudest snore in the world. The show got about 25 viewers but it was worth all the effort and, for years, I was more proud of it than of anything else,' he says.

He also cited his strong working relationships with several key actors and directors, all of which would hold him in good stead when he tried to win the show some big interviews. Actor Johnny Depp had become an increasingly good friend, while he and Jane had both spent an evening in an LA strip club getting to know Nicolas Cage far better than most. David Lynch, director of *The Elephant Man* and *Wild at Heart*, was also close, both professionally as well as personally. 'He's great,' says Jonathan. 'He was the subject of the first programme I was ever part of as a researcher. He then joined me on *The Last Resort* one night and I made a full profile of him that was shown at the end of 1990. Even by then I think we had built up a good rapport.'

And while it had been almost entirely overlooked due to awful scheduling, he also pointed to the late-night arts review show *Mondo Rosso* that he had made in the mid-1990s as proof of his dedication to film. It had included a lengthy discussion of cult movies with guests such as Vic Reeves and Jarvis Cocker. Jonathan had also tried to turn the previously dry and academic world of film publishing on its head in the early 1990s by researching and writing his typically irreverent *The Incredibly Strange Film Book* to tie in with his television show. When it comes to films, Jonathan felt, he had form and he had paid his dues.

Fortunately, BBC Controller Peter Salmon, the man who publicly announced Jonathan's new role, was incredibly supportive as the debate over his man's suitability raged. 'Jonathan has stepped into some big shoes but we know they will fit him comfortably,' he said in an unplanned damage-limitation exercise. 'We wanted to find popular television's new face of film and there is no one more qualified for that role than him.'

Barry Norman also said he was delighted at the BBC's choice as his replacement – though, when he said it was 'keeping it in the family', a few of the accusations of nepotism that Jonathan had been dreading did start to surface. Barry's other comment was that he hoped Jonathan's near-obsessive passion for film didn't one day cause problems in his new role. The veteran was well known for thinking the BBC no longer cared much about films and didn't really value the show. 'I wish Jonathan well but I don't know if he has yet found a niche for himself,' were his final words on the subject. 'When somebody starts a new job, you can't say how they are going to be at it. He might be no good at all...'

Jonathan, of course, was determined to prove the old man wrong. This was the job he felt he had been born to do and the role he had spent years secretly preparing for. Now, at last, it was showtime.

Barry's old chair was thrown out in a minor revamp, to be replaced by a slick black-leather sofa. The location also changed – production was moved to a purpose-built studio in Maida Vale. But Jonathan was adamant that the iconic theme tune should stay and he didn't want too many changes to the basic format and style of the show either – even though many at the BBC wanted to throw some even more dramatic innovations into the mix.

Jonathan was prepared to see more in-studio interviews and analysis, but he said his overall focus would be viewer-friendly commentary. He preferred a useful review, rather than an academic criticism, and some trademark humour. He also wanted to broaden the range of the programme. 'One of the things I feel all TV film programming misses out on is the love of the trashier end of the spectrum. I don't mean mad old B-movies; I mean the films that tend to be the most popular with the viewing public. The big popcorn-laden blockbusters.'

What he didn't want to do was cheapen the brand, which triggered a battle royal when the show's producers said they wanted to film some trailers for the new series featuring Jonathan, for reasons that have since been forgotten, in his bath. He refused point-blank and a tense period of brinkmanship ensued. 'I feel quite within my rights to say what I do and don't feel comfortable doing,' he said at the time. 'If people liked the show when Barry Norman was doing it and then they see me sitting in a bath, what would they think? The show is about movies, not about me. I'm fighting for the integrity of the thing. I'm conscious of the disastrous potential of me looking like I have gone nuts. Barry always treated this show with respect and I intend to do just the same. I want to bring my own style to this, so it is a different show, but I want it to be still recognisable to all the long-term viewers.'

This sentiment was surprisingly mature, coming from a performer more known for his irreverence and a healthy disrespect for the rules. But Jonathan had a long-term plan for what was then *Film '99*. If he got his way, this would be more than a short-term filler programme to pay for school fees or a new beach house. It would be much more. 'I am more excited about this than I have been about any television role in years. I can't imagine ever getting bored with movies. I want to beat Barry Norman's record. I want to be doing *Film '25*. I want to die in that seat.'

What he was also determined to do was to pass on his huge enthusiasm for films of all types. He said his overall aim on *Film '99* was to be positive – though he wouldn't hold back from ripping bad films to pieces should they need it. 'I'm not ashamed to admit that I really enjoy some terrible movies and watch them endlessly,' he admitted when he began running through his personal high- and lowlights. 'One of them is Paul Verhoeven's *Showgirls*, about Las Vegas strippers. It's awful but great at the same time. It's the perfect mix of trash meets trash – the subject matter deserves nothing more. There's an awful lot of nudity in it, but it is incredibly dull by the end. I never thought I would find myself looking away from the screen when there are bare breasts on it. But by the time you get to the 400th pair of boobs, you're thinking, "Oh no, not another set!" and getting ready to fast-forward.'

Over the years, Jonathan has certainly built up an eclectic mix of films that he loves, and films he loves to hate. Determined never to be a film snob, he says he doesn't mind being shamelessly manipulated by moviemakers – as long as they do the job well. *ET*, he says, is a classic example. 'Spielberg's direction was masterful. He just tapped into one human emotion and used it, amplified it. I think some people who saw the movie reacted against that and, consequently, didn't enjoy the film. I certainly wasn't one of them.'

Blade Runner continues to be one of his all-time favourites. 'There's such a terrific look to it that I could watch it over and over again. It almost single-handedly created a vision of the future with buildings going higher and trash cans on street corners. The first time I saw it, I was completely blown away,' he says.

A lot further from the mainstream comes a less likely favourite – Russ Meyer's *Faster Pussycat! Kill! Kill!*. 'Jane and I are both huge fans of Russ Meyer. This sixties movie starts with go-go dancers and sordid men going, "Faster, pussycat, faster!" Then there's this deep voice which intones, "Woman... the most dangerous breed there is." Murder, mayhem and desert chases follow. It's terrific.'

A little-known Japanese film made back in 1952 is also one of Jonathan's top films. He says *Ikiru* – which follows a man diagnosed with cancer, who realises he has wasted his life and decides to create a children's playground in his last few months – is incredibly poignant. 'The final shot of him sitting on a swing, singing a song to himself as the snow falls, gives me goosebumps,' Jonathan says. He reckons *The Lavender Hill Mob* is one of the best ever British comedies, says *It's A Wonderful Life* always makes him cry, and is also a big fan of Fellini's *8½*.

Some surprising modern and mainstream films also get two thumbs-up from him. *Dumb & Dumber* is one of them. 'I do like poor-taste films,' he says unapologetically. 'When Jim Carrey sells the budgie to the blind boy – it's my favourite bit.' Finally, among his favourites, is *Groundhog Day*. 'I love feel-good movies which communally lift an audience. As everyone walks out of the cinema, we all feel warmer towards each other. Bill Murray is excellent, and Jane and I both love the film.'

Arty films which try to be clever but end up being

pretentious are in his hall of shame. And he cites Madonna's *Body of Evidence* as proof that, when people set out to make deliberately sexy films, they almost always end up doing the opposite. He was, however, fully prepared to defend the one major film he had appeared in – *Spiceworld*, which came out in 1997. While joking that he took the role (as himself) variously for the money and to please his Spice Girls-obsessed daughter Betty, he continues to argue that the film will one day be seen as a classic of its self-mocking British pop genre. Though, to date, he is unsure of exactly when that 'one day' might come.

If you want to prove that success really does breed success, then Jonathan's career in early 1999 can be used as the ultimate example. Starting work on Barry Norman's old show meant that the movie-lover in him had never been happier. And all of a sudden, his inner television nerd was about to feel just as satisfied. Jonathan was asked to be the host of a new comedy panel show called *It's Only TV But I Like It*.

Also on board as the captains of two competing teams were Jack Dee and Julian Clary. It was a trio that certainly raised eyebrows in the incestuous world of television – because Jonathan, Jack and Julian all had business links with the same manager, Addison Cresswell. Getting them all on the same BBC show was seen as a financial masterstroke for all concerned – and there were a lot of green faces at the Groucho Club when the show's well-paid line-up was announced.

The series itself started well. Stars-of-the-moment

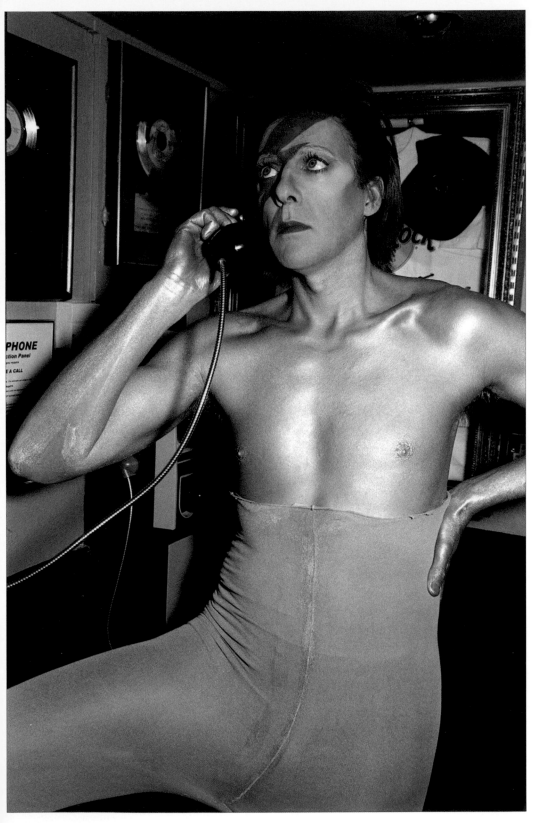

Jonathan waits to be put through to a starman, waiting in the sky.

The (karma) chameleon-like Jonathan Ross does a Boy George at the singer's 40th birthday party, accompanied by Jane.

Top: It's Suity Spice! Checking out the Spice Girls at the height of their success outside the Albert Hall in 1997.

Bottom: How much talent? Big, big talent as Jonathan makes opportunity knock for a bunch of young hopefuls.

Top: Sean Bean and Ulrika Jonsson join the select band of millions who have seen the Ross undergarments.

Middle: It's not Derek and Clive, it's David (Baddiel) and Jonathan, performing at a tribute to Peter Cook on stage in 2002.

Bottom: *Pop Idol* Simon Cowell sees the funny side at the 2003 Comedy Awards with Jonathan.

Friday Night With Jonathan Ross won the Best Comedy Entertainment Programme at the Comedy Awards in 2003.

Top: With cricketer Phil Tufnell on *They Think It's All Over*.

Bottom left: Nice pair of Baftas – Jane and Jonathan celebrate his win in 2004.

Bottom right: Betty Kitten, Honey Kinny, Jane Goldman, Harvey Kirby and Jonathan at a premiere in London's fashionable Leicester Square.

Joining the Ugly Sisterhood in the sound recording of *Shrek 2*.

Jonathan Ross, broadcaster and OBE, at Buckingham Palace in November 2005.

Caroline Aherne, Ant and Dec and Antony Worrall Thompson were the guests on the first show and ratings reflected the high profile of everyone concerned.

What made life even better for Jonathan as *It's Only TV But I Like It* was aired was the fact that, back at home, he wasn't the only one to be paid handsomely for indulging in his hobbies. Jane had found a way to make money from one of her favourite passions as well – American theme parks and white-knuckle roller-coaster rides. The idea had come to her several years earlier when a guide at Disney World in Florida had shown the family some of the secret underground tunnels that get staff and supplies around the park without affecting the guests. 'My immediate thought when I saw them was: "Something horrible could happen under here and no one would ever know." That gave me the idea for a book,' says Jane.

Back at the Florida house, and back in Britain, Jane started to work on some characters and a plot. And she realised she might have hit upon something very special. Countless conspiracy theories exist about how theme park owners try to hush up accidental deaths on their premises to protect their precious images. Jane was convinced she could harness all that into a brilliant thriller. What made it slightly more fun was that she and Jonathan decided they needed to thoroughly research the market she would be writing about. 'We used our children as an excuse and dragged them around endless theme parks, so it is a good job they love them as much as we do,' Jane said as she began work on the manuscript. *Dreamworld*, billed as a 'darkly comic thriller', followed a Florida park's security guard's growing realisation that there was trouble in her artfully created paradise. There was a huge amount of detail about the secrets that park companies keep from their customers and the lengths to which they would go to protect their pristine images.

'Jane is definitely a talent and she could easily be a top novelist. Her writing is superb and there are some great twists and turns in the book,' said her HarperCollins editor Susan Opie after the manuscript was completed on time in early 1999. The plan was to publish it the following summer and there were hopes that the film rights could be sold for several hundred thousand pounds. Jonathan arranged for a babysitter and took Jane out for a meal near their home in Hampstead to celebrate and, as they started to count their blessings, they realised it was difficult to know where to stop.

What made Jonathan so pleased was that his entire extraordinary family was doing well. He and Jane had recently headed back to a pub theatre in Leytonstone to see his mother, Martha, in a play his stepdad, Tony Phillips, had written. Called *The Firm's Big Night Out*, it also starred former *EastEnders* actor Peter Dean. Almost the entire Ross clan had been in the audience – and all of them had been on top form. Amazingly, every one of the Ross children had travelled a long way from their 'five boys to a room' childhoods. And all had made successful careers in the entertainment industry.

Simon had set up his own production company, making, among many other shows, a new series for Richard and Judy. Back then, Miles was branching out from television to film production, working on the Lee Evans and Nathan Lane comedy *MouseHunt*. Adam was acting, working as a session musician and writing screenplays. Lisa, who had also been in television, was taking time out to raise her three children but was planning to launch an acting school as soon as they were old enough to manage without her during the day. Older brother Paul, meanwhile, had become ubiquitous. Paul had led Jonathan into the television world and made a name for himself as a safe pair of hands behind the camera as a producer on *The Six O'Clock Show* and *The London Programme*, but he had long since decided to have some fun in front of the lens. He launched a new career as a presenter – and his little brother Jonathan loved to joke that he would present just about anything.

'The message on your answering machine doesn't say hello. It just says, "Yes, I'll do it," you big media tart,' Jonathan would laugh at him. But, jokes aside, he was the first to applaud his big brother's stamina. In a three-year period in the late 1990s, Paul appeared on more than 500 editions of game shows like *Jeopardy*, *Endurance UK*, *All of the Shop* and *Life's a Punt*. He also made a splash in two six-month stints opposite Paula Yates on *The Big Breakfast*. Most of it was unashamedly lowbrow stuff, but the Ross family had never been embarrassed about that. And sibling rivalry was never a big problem for any of them. 'We're ferociously defensive of each other. We can say anything to each other, but no one else can,' says Paul. 'We are also all for nepotism. We're like the Dimblebys on acid. We're the Corleones of British television. If you can't trust your brother, who can you trust? Jonathan is Fredo, the ratty one. Simon is Michael, the cool one. I'm Sonny, the hothead who acts before he thinks. We were brought up to think, "My brother's triumph is my triumph", and we're not jealous because none of us really values material things,' says Paul. 'We're too laidback for that and, when we get together, which we do all the time, we talk about family. We don't talk about work.'

But one other thing the whole family, and everyone else, was talking about back then was the bizarre rumour about Jonathan, Jane and a supposed night of passion with a mysterious Hollywood star. The story centred around an incident that had allegedly taken place a few months earlier at the annual *Comedy Awards* ceremony. Looking back, Jonathan admits he gave the gossips plenty to go on by joking about it for far too long afterwards.

He had sown the first seeds of the story when he had been asked to contribute to a television documentary about fidelity. Talking about his own ten-year marriage, he said that a major American star at the awards ceremony had, he thought, become increasingly flirtatious with him backstage – although he admits that his late-start romantic development meant he was no expert in recognising or responding to such behaviour.

He also refused to say who the star was, although he did give a few clues. 'She was an internationally famous person whom I had always found quite sexy when young – and she was still quite sexy,' he hinted. And, when the awards show was finally over and the cameras stopped rolling, he said he thought her advances had become even clearer. The star had a suite in the same five-star London hotel where the ceremony had taken place; as did Jonathan. It seemed that he was told to forget about his own room and head on over to hers, which is where the story got even more interesting.

Jonathan didn't follow the star. Instead, he went back to his own suite where Jane was waiting for him... and he told her everything that had happened. Jonathan being Jonathan, and Jane being Jane, the whole story was treated as a huge joke. At first, both sat open-mouthed as they thought through the implications of what he thought had just happened – and then they both started to laugh.

'Maybe I should do it. It is so-and-so, after all,' is how Jonathan remembers the joke developing.

'Well, seeing as it is so-and-so, if you really want to do it, go ahead and do it,' is what he said Jane had replied.

And, of course, he then admitted that he didn't want to and they forgot all about it. Or at least they did until the fidelity documentary was screened, the story broke, and newspaper headlines screamed about: 'MY WIFE SAID "YES" TO MY CELEBRITY AFFAIR' and 'JONATHAN: WHY JANE SAYS I'M FREE TO SLEEP AROUND'.

Realising that the joke had gone too far, Jane called some reporters to try to set the record straight. Everyone admits they have no idea if the star in question had actually propositioned Jonathan or if her natural friendliness had been misconstrued. More importantly, Jane was determined to get the message across that she had never given Jonathan permission for a one-night stand, let alone an affair.

'The whole story was ridiculous, but, for the record, no, I did not give him permission to sleep with anyone else,' she was forced to say as the rumour mill ground on. 'Ours is a solid relationship forged by the fact that neither of us has ever done anything to hurt the other. The story was a joke and the funny thing is that Jonathan would never even think anyone thought he was attractive, let alone brag about something like that. The thought of him striding into a room and demanding my permission to sleep with someone is hilarious.'

For his part, Jonathan admitted that, for all his bravado, he had no interest in sleeping around – and, even if he did, it wouldn't be with a Hollywood beauty. Having been up close and personal with so many of the world's most beautiful women, Jonathan is ready to destroy most of their male fans' illusions and say the women are normally a big turn-off. 'It's not normal to be that perfect, is it? I don't actually find it appealing and can't imagine it can be that much fun sleeping with people who are more worried about what they look like than what they are doing. No one is going to enjoy themselves when that's what's going on.'

In spite of the jokes he made on the fidelity documentary, Jonathan's private thoughts on affairs and promiscuity are a lot more serious, not least because he simply doesn't believe that Casanovas whose little black books resemble telephone directories are really having much more fun. 'Does it get much different when you get up to 100 partners?' he asks rhetorically. 'I would have thought that the increased volume would decrease it being special. I would have thought that it would make it more mundane, as opposed to somehow better or more exciting. I also don't think that sex with random individuals is ever going to be that different, that special, an event. And after the event, I think you are going to feel pretty much like, well, that was fun, sure, but was it that much more fun than doing it with the person you have chosen to be with for the rest of your life? For my part, my attitude towards Jane has always been: "This is not the person who is standing between me and a good time. This is the person I want to have all those good times with." And I would have to suffer a personality disorder not to find Jane the sexiest woman alive.'

The final comment proved that, for all his traditional views about the sanctity of marriage, Jonathan was very far from being a prude. In fact, he was happy to talk about sex at almost any opportunity – and he was always ready to focus on his own, hopefully Olympian, performance.

'I can't begin to tell you how much I like sex,' he told *Sunday Mirror* reporter Sharon Feinstein. 'It's my favourite thing in the world, a huge source of constant pleasure. I think about it hundreds of times a day and do it whenever possible. I shoot for it every night. I know I won't get it every night, but, if you don't shoot for it, you are going to regret it. If I haven't had sex for a night, it starts to get on top of me. But I can go without it providing there's the promise of it for the next night. As long as there's a carrot dangling in front of this particular donkey, then he's quite happy.'

He nicknamed Jane 'Foxy' and loved jokingly to

embarrass her by hyping up stories of their passion. 'By day, she is like a wonderful, refined character from a Jane Austen novel. By night, she is as wild as I could possibly hope for.' And Jonathan didn't stop at talking about how much he likes sex. He was prepared to talk about the details of it as well. 'I've become a very good lover,' he claims with a smile. 'I put a lot of effort into it and Jane seems really happy and satisfied. I'm very dedicated to the craft and, if there were prizes to be given out, I would be short-listed. I'm not selfish. I hope I'm reasonably thoughtful. I just so much enjoy being part of the act and being in the moment that I'm quite happy for it to go on as long as possible. I'm not perfect by any means, but I am very happy with all parts of my body. Some of them are absolutely breathtaking. What can I say? God was good to me. I've got a Viagra tablet at home that a friend bought for me from a stag night in New York. I have no plans to use it.'

It was good stuff, from a man approaching his tenth wedding anniversary in 1999. And even this event was celebrated in typically offbeat style. Jonathan decided to take Jane and the whole family out for a romantic lunch. They headed out of London and went for a long country walk before arriving at their favourite restaurant. Once inside, they were led to their table, sat down and ordered their meal. Then Jonathan produced his masterstroke. 'We had brought a Walkman for each child and we just plugged them in. Honey had a Barney tape, Harvey had something from Nickelodeon and Betty had The Spice Girls. It was the first time Jane and I had had a proper conversation during the day in ages,' he says.

Heading back into London after such a wonderful day out, Jonathan was once again unable to stop counting his blessings. He had a wonderful wife whom he loved and who still inspired and supported him; they had three wonderful children, two wonderful homes, plenty of money in the bank and careers that they both hugely enjoyed. He held his wife's hand tightly as they walked towards their front door and prepared for another quiet night in. Jonathan, in particular, was feeling incredibly confident about the future. Winter was about to turn to spring and Jonathan was convinced they were going to have the best year of their lives. He could hardly have been more wrong.

10

Breaking Point

Jonathan has been immensely proud of his wife's ebullience and individuality ever since they first met in Stringfellow's back in 1987. He loved it every time her unique spirit was recognised by the newspapers and Jane got the credit for being a good mother and a strong role model for other women. But, in the late 1990s, this kind of positive coverage was becoming increasingly thin on the ground. Jonathan would go through the papers in his office at home, or in his dressing room at the BBC, and quite literally groan when he read some of the latest catty comments about his wife.

The descriptions of Jane's fashion choices didn't bother him – not least because the papers were equally brutal about him. So he was able to laugh when one female reporter called Jane 'Lara Croft meets Barbarella... Ginger Spice meets Hedy Lamarr... Rachel Weisz in a tangle with a thrift-shop bargain bucket... Vivienne Westwood model turned Camden Lock stallholder'. He didn't mind when another paper wrote, 'She's a mother of three in her thirties, but she acts like she's a teenager,' because that was precisely why he loved her.

Other descriptions were far less flattering. It was when Jonathan sat preparing for an episode of *It's Only TV But I Like It* one afternoon that he saw Jane described as 'the Jessica Rabbit wife of Jonathan Ross, a glam-goth floozie, happy to just hang out in the green room and giggle at her husband's jokes'. Around the same time, Boy George's autobiography came out, in which he referred to 'Jane Gold-digger' after she got married. Jonathan was worried that these kinds of comments were starting to hit home. He knew Jane was increasingly tired as she struggled to finish the manuscript for *Dreamworld*.

Jane had come down with chicken pox when she was eight months' pregnant with Betty and, two years later, had been hospitalised after the painful gall bladder infection when she was on a tight deadline to complete her first *X-Files* book. She had suffered a miscarriage between their first and second children and had needed Jonathan to give her daily injections of progesterone when she was pregnant with Harvey and they were living in a rented flat in LA. Back in Britain, Jane has also been a long-term sufferer of SAD, Seasonal Affective Disorder, which made her feel lethargic and low in the grey, cold months of every autumn and winter.

As if all this wasn't bad enough, the simple fact of having three children in little more than five years had left her exhausted, not least because, while the couple had taken on a part-time housekeeper to try to help organise their domestic lives, they were determined never to farm out their children to a full-time nanny. They juggled the childcare around their work and the help that their respective parents could offer.

Looking back, Jonathan admits that he hadn't helped first by unburdening himself on to her with all his career and financial worries around the time he had left Generation X, and then by temporarily clamming up and freezing Jane out when he tried to find a new direction afterwards. His own mood swings and inability to express his feelings didn't help either. 'When I was away from Jane, even for a day, I always thought of her with love,' he says. 'But back then when she was around, I probably acted as if I sometimes found her quite irritating, which I think would have worn anyone out.'

Equally debilitating was the fact that the pair continued to have frequent humdingers of arguments – although Jonathan admits that these could make them both laugh as much as cry. On one occasion, he says, they were rowing in the kitchen late at night over something neither of them can remember. And, in order to make some seemingly important point, he picked up the nearest thing he could find and flung it at the wall. In a soap opera or Hollywood film, that something might have been a glass, a plate or even a vase, producing a grand, dramatic gesture as it shattered into a thousand pieces. But in Jonathan's case the nearest thing he had to hand was an over-ripe watermelon and, when it hit the wall, it splattered into a mass of fleshy innards, pips, juice and gloop. Both Jonathan and Jane started laughing hysterically as they watched the mess spread over their kitchen units and trickle down on to the floor. The argument was over. They were happy again.

One March evening in 1999, that happiness was to take a real battering, however. Jonathan and Jane had gone out for a quiet dinner with friends, leaving their children with a babysitter. During the evening, an intruder climbed through a half-open window at the back of their house. The babysitter heard a noise at about 10.00pm, went to investigate and disturbed the lone burglar on the stairs. Fortunately, he fled immediately and the sitter rang Jonathan and Jane's mobile and the police, as she rushed upstairs to check on the children. 'It wasn't a nice experience and I don't want to talk about it,' Jonathan told reporters the next day.

It turned out that their house hadn't been targeted specifically – two neighbours' houses had also been broken into that evening with cash stolen from one of them. 'We believe it was an opportunistic thief who thought the property was empty,' a police spokesman said as an investigation was launched.

Jane, in particular, had been unable to sleep on the night of the break-in. After rushing home with Jonathan to check on the children, she had spent a sleepless night worrying about how much worse the incident could have been. And it was far from the first sleepless night she had endured in recent months. As her workload and her parental responsibilities grew in the late 1990s, it began to get out of control. Jane looked after the family in the day, and wrote long into the night when everyone else was asleep. She says, at one point, the very thought of going to sleep reminded her of going under general anaesthetic – and subconsciously she stopped herself from doing it. 'Ultimately, I was so sleep-deprived I couldn't think straight. I thought I was going mad. Every few days, I would be so overcome by exhaustion that I would crash out in the afternoon for a few hours and that was it. That was all the sleep I was getting,' she says. A death in her family, coming so soon after the burglary attempt and another long period of sleepless nights, just made matters worse. It was as if fate was throwing as many bad experiences as possible at Jane to see if she might snap.

April mornings on Hampstead Heath can be bracing affairs. High above the rest of London, a cold, wet wind can whip across the near 800-acre expanse of greenery and woods as the capital's dog walkers and joggers hurry by. Almost all of the back windows of the Ross house give a view of this fantastic, ever-changing scene. Look out and in the distance you can see some of the regulars pulling their coats a little tighter as they stop to chat. Or perhaps you can see some of the hopeful new runners being beaten by the heath's surprisingly steep hills. But, one morning in early April 1999, you would have seen something else as well; something deeply disturbing.

The family's housekeeper Kate was the first to notice. Far beyond the garden fence, she spotted a lone but familiar figure. It looked as if Jane had slipped out on the heath, taking an early-morning walk in what seemed to be a pair of cotton pyjamas. Clearly, something was very wrong. Kate grabbed a coat and rushed out to fetch her employer and bring her back into the warm, dry house. 'I genuinely lost the plot. I was in a daze, a horrible, horrible state to be in,' Jane said of that awful morning.

She and Jonathan spent the rest of the day sitting at home trying to work out what was going on. Both cried a little, and both tried to be as open, honest and supportive as they could be. Jane needed Jonathan like never before, and he wouldn't let her down. He got on the phone to doctors, therapists, friends and relatives to gather information about their next move. With help, things slowly came together again and she seemed on course for a full recovery. But, as it turned out, there was one more terrifying event still to happen, one more crisis still to be overcome.

This final hurdle occurred when the whole family headed south to stay in a hotel near Poole in Dorset. The idea was to have a relaxing couple of days together to focus on all the good things in their lives and work as a stepping-stone towards a more stable future. But a freak accident was to plunge them all back into crisis. The weather was wonderfully good that early summer weekend and the family decided to have a picnic in the countryside. They bought food at the local supermarket, laughing and having fun as they pushed the trolley round the aisles and allowing everyone their favourite treats. Then they drove off to find the perfect spot, laid out some blankets in the sun and began their feast. Later in the afternoon, Jonathan and Jane lay back in the grass talking softly, as the children kicked off their shoes and played games around them. It was magical, memorable, wonderful stuff and it was easy to feel that nothing bad in life could ever happen again. Or it was until two-year-old Honey screamed.

Rushing towards her, Jonathan and Jane found she had been bitten by a snake – an adder. Adders, which can be up to 2 feet long, are Britain's only poisonous snake, and as Honey found they are all the more terrifying by the speed at which they can move and the sinister V-shaped marks on their heads. Bites are rare, with only a dozen reported most years, but when they happen they cause intense pain and they can, of course, kill. Honey, not surprisingly, was in a terrible state – as were her parents.

The family rushed her to Poole General Hospital where Honey was treated with drugs for the potentially lethal bite. 'An adder bite is not necessarily going to be fatal but for a small child it is, of course, very dangerous and very, very frightening,' one of the hospital doctors told the media afterwards. The doctors said Honey had to stay in hospital overnight for observation, not least because the antidotes to adder bites can in themselves cause bad reactions in some patients.

Taking turns by her bedside, Jonathan and Jane tried to reassure their other two children and cope with their own secret fears. It was the very worst possible end to the family's dream weekend in the country, but, when it was over, it turned out to have helped rather than hindered Jane's recovery process.

'Jonathan, poor thing, had been under so much pressure, he was beside himself,' Jane remembers. 'He was so upset that I ended up dealing with this family trauma. And I thought, "This is terrible and stressful but I'm coping and I think I'm OK." And we could all see light at the end of the tunnel at last.' What they didn't know was that it was still a deceptively long tunnel.

After a long and horrible night, Honey was given the all clear by the doctors and the family tried to keep their spirits up on the drive home. Jane to get get better and learn how to maintain her equilibrium in any future crises. One thing she was told was that bottling problems up was almost always going to be a problem. Talk is good, psychologists say. But what they didn't say was that it can also be a problem if, like Jonathan and Jane, you live in the public eye.

They'd also seen problems in the lives of those around them. Jonathan's parents split up after four decades of apparently happy marriage and what felt at the time like ever-more permanent fractures in his brother Paul's relationship were even more disturbing.

Jonathan's problem with seeing his big brother in trouble wasn't just that Paul was still a role model to him. It was also the fact that the way Paul described meeting his wife Kerry was so similar to the way Jonathan had met Jane. 'I loved Kerry from the first time I set eyes on her across a smoky old coffee machine at London Weekend Television when I was a surly researcher and she was a PA,' Paul says in a rare moment of seriousness. Jonathan says he loved Jane from the first time he saw her in an even smokier Stringfellow's. Paul's recent affairs with a TV researcher and another glamorous blonde had led to him being dubbed a 'serial adulterer' by the media. And, when he was snapped kissing Caroline Aherne at a drunken awards ceremony, he had the label 'love rat' applied to him as well.

Desperate to understand his brother, help his family and seek personal reassurance, Jonathan spoke endlessly to Paul on the phone. And, as it turned out, Paul was able to tell his brother what he needed to hear. His message was simple – that the best relationships can survive the biggest of shocks. Paul accepted that many people might be surprised that he and Kerry were still living under the same roof after so many problems, but Jonathan shouldn't be. 'Kerry and I care about each other. We've got four children and we have been together since 1984. We're talking about 15 years since we first met. That's a long history to throw away. To Kerry's credit, and mine, neither of us has stopped working at our marriage.' This was just what Jonathan needed to know. It was the shot in the arm that could see him through the rest of 1999, and it was an essential piece of life support because fate still had a lot more to throw at him.

As the new, carefully selected host of *Film '99*, Jonathan didn't just have to be at Cannes; he had to schmooze and shine there as well. It would be when his credentials as the nation's number-one film buff would be tested, publicly, for the first time. And it would be when the critics would line up to say he should never have got Barry Norman's job if he failed.

So Jane steeled herself, painted on a smile and headed

down to the South of France with her husband. At MTV's paparazzi-filled all-night beach party, she certainly didn't disappoint. She pulled a glistening frock coat over a leopardskin bikini, pulled a black cowboy hat over her shocking, ever-pinker hair and headed down the red carpet on Jonathan's arm. The paparazzi went wild. Not only were they getting shots of that summer's hottest couple in celeb-land, but they were getting some of the most eye-catching images of the year as well. Jane Goldman, Jonathan's wild and wonderful wife, was back. Simply being there and standing so close to her husband sent out some powerful messages. Mission accomplished, it meant that Jonathan could focus 100 per cent on his day job and talk about film to his heart's content.

The bosses at the BBC were overjoyed and Jonathan says he had a ball. That year's big mainstream film was the sleeper hit *The Blair Witch Project*, which Jonathan and Jane both loved. Other Hollywood films included *Dogma* and *Entrapment*, while the couple were also over the moon to be able to see so many of the offbeat European and world cinema screenings that dominate the festival. With everyone from Holly Hunter and Kristen Scott Thomas to David Cronenberg and Jeff Goldblum to hang out with – as well as Pedro Almodóvar, one of the couple's long-loved favourite directors – the Cannes trip looked set to go down as a complete success.

Back in Britain, while Jonathan filmed some follow-up strands for the next set of *Film '99* shows, the Rosses were under as much pressure as ever. No more watermelons had been thrown, but a lot of insults and accusations had been bouncing off their Hampstead walls late into the night. As the tensions threatened once more to get out of control, the couple realised that these were desperate times – and that they called for the most desperate of measures. Jane had recently said that her greatest fear in life was 'to be separated from Jonathan and the children, even temporarily'. But she was about to enforce just such a separation upon herself. She decided to move out of the marital home – Jonathan was staying behind with the children. No one had any idea what would happen next.

11

Split Personalities

To this day, it is unclear who tipped off the media about this latest crisis surrounding the couple's marriage. But the sudden arrival of a pack of photographers outside their front door in Hampstead proved that the news was out. A barrage of flashes and clicks went off as Jane left the house and headed to the rented flat she had found on the other side of the village. In their cruel and intrusive way, every paper, it seemed, wanted a picture of Jane crying. But, as she kissed Jonathan on the cheek and rushed towards her car, it looked as if he might be the one in tears. This very public tragedy had not yet lost its capacity to surprise.

Jane's new flat, which she described as 'bleak and lonely', was less than a mile from the marital home. But it could just as well have been in another world. Without his wife, Jonathan knew the family home was starting to feel just as alien. The one positive thing, and the key reason for Jane's move, was that the house was now quiet. Both admitted that the passionate, sometimes strangely refreshing rows which had punctuated their relationship in its early days had recently taken a very different tone. They had acquired a harder and far more brutal edge. Everything was about breaking up rather than making up. There was no humour, only danger. And, while all their previous rows had been confined to times when their children were asleep or out of the house, it seemed as if they could now occur at any time. And neither Jonathan nor Jane wanted anyone else dragged down with them. Both had heard too many stories about how children can have their lives destroyed if they grow up in angry, violent homes. Jonathan and Jane had both been spared that in their own happy childhoods, so they were damned if they were going to inflict it on their own kids.

What they had also wanted to do was to keep this crisis in private and under wraps to protect the children further. But, after a while, they realised that their public lives meant this was never going to be allowed to happen. Instead, they would have to try and explain what was going on with as much dignity as possible and hope that the media would leave them alone.

Neil Reading, Jonathan's long-term spokesman, was called upon to make an official statement. 'As a result of a very stressful period, a great deal of strain has been put on the marriage. Jane and Jonathan's main concern at the moment is the happiness and security of their children. They want to ensure their children's routine remains disrupted as little as possible. The couple would like to stress their current living arrangements are strictly a practical, temporary measure and the two remain very close and love one another very much. Divorce is out of the question.'

As it turned out, the reporters did not then leave the couple alone and Jane was ultimately forced to give more details. She decided to be harrowingly honest about the pressures the couple were under. 'I had to move out because we had been rowing and arguing so much at that point,' Jane said. 'Most importantly, we didn't ever want to fight in front of the kids. And, when we had some really horrendous fights, I could feel it was destroying what we had. We're both hideously dirty fighters... very below the belt. It has all been immensely stressful for Jonathan. He was great, but I think he really needed support and I had been unable to give him any. We are doing this now to make sure this situation need never arise again.'

Fortunately, it was a particularly civilised separation. Jane came back to the family home every morning to help make the children's breakfasts and was there most days to pick them up from school, read them stories and look after them in the evenings before disappearing quietly back to her flat. She spent much of each weekend at the family home as well. As far as the children were concerned, just as she and Jonathan had hoped, it was pretty much business as usual.

Those who know the couple closest were also certain that the separation was indeed just a temporary measure. 'They always get on well and I am sure they have a future together,' Jane's dad Stuart Goldman said when reporters tracked him down and asked him about his daughter's marriage.

'This is not the end, nor is it even the beginning of the end,' said friends. 'It is simply a necessary stepping-stone, a short period of breathing space in a lengthy marriage which will ultimately last much, much longer.'

Reading the newspapers – which Jonathan was forced to do in order to keep his jokes topical at work – told a different story, however. As usual, a host of experts were being asked for their opinions and very few of them were good. Julia Cole, a therapist and counsellor with relationship-guidance service Relate, was asked about the couple's age gap and the fact that Jane had married so young. 'You are a very different person at 27 than you were at 17,' she concluded. 'The person you choose for a husband as a teenager might not be the one you see as a life partner when you get older.'

It was not in any way what Jonathan wanted to read. As if this wasn't bad enough, Rod Stewart and Rachel Hunter were also splitting up. Rod and Rachel had also long since claimed that their relationship would survive their big age gap. If it couldn't, the commentators suggested, then Jane and Jonathan would suffer a similar fate. But here, at last, came some good news. Those who knew them well said there was a world of difference between the two couples, and one of Jonathan's friends was prepared to go very public about it.

'Two celebrity marriages, two identical reasons for breaking up. But there ends the similarity between the two separations,' said author, columnist and friend Jane

Moore. 'Like Rachel, Jane was very young when she married and had children. Now she feels she has missed out and needs some time to herself. But, unlike Rachel, Jane is married to a class act who understands her problems and doesn't place his ego above all else.' Jane Moore said that she had spotted the warning signs during a recent heart-to-heart chat with Jonathan. 'He said, "When I met Jane, I was a young 26 and she was a mature 16. But I think we have both changed a lot recently. In the early days, neither of us noticed the age gap, but we are more aware of it now. I am beginning to be conscious of the ageing process and, at 28, Jane feels she is in the last flush of youth." Jonathan clearly knew the storm clouds were brewing but, unlike Rod Stewart, he will do everything he can to make sure the sunnier times return,' Jane Moore concluded. 'He is a completely different calibre of husband. He will be feeling very real and deep pain about his marital problems but his love for his young wife is so great he's prepared to give her whatever space she needs. He won't pressurise her and he certainly won't let his ego get in the way of a possible reconciliation. He knows she has spent the past ten years being a support act to his seesawing career. Now it's her time to have a bit of breathing space.'

This turned out to be exactly what happened. Being away from her family in her bleak and lonely flat gave Jane the time she needed to think.

Back at the family home, Jonathan found a new perspective as well, and both were ultimately able to find a common ground. After less than a month apart, Jane shut and locked the door on her rented flat. The lease was paid until the end of the year but she never wanted to see it again. She was heading home. Everything was going to be good again – and the couple decided to go public about their new start in typical style. They were going out to a friend's party just after their reconciliation and knew the media would be there in force to see whether they looked and acted like the flamboyantly happy couple of old. So they decided to put on quite a show.

Jonathan chose a blazingly eye-catching leopardskin suit when they headed out of the house. Jane, touchingly, had a matching leopardskin handbag. They held hands all the way down the street and looked fantastic together. 'Yes, I've moved back in. We are really happy together and we have worked through all our troubles,' Jane told reporters as the couple got into their car amidst the media scrum.

A few weeks later, when more of the dust had settled and life in the Ross household was truly calm again, Jane was confident enough to say more. 'The great thing about the time we spent apart was that we both missed each other so much,' she began. 'And I don't think there was ever a time when we really considered actually splitting up. To go through something horrible and to come out the other side and find that your life is fantastic is a wonderful thing and I feel very, very grateful. To have Jonathan, and the children, and a job I love... it feels like a fresh start.

'I used to have a huge fear of embarrassing myself. I never wanted to admit that anything had gone wrong or that I had made a bad decision about even the smallest thing. I suppose I had some desire to seem as if I had always done the right thing and that everything was perfect in my life. Even when I was bullied at school, I never told because I wanted everyone to think that everything was all right.' And so, in a strange but important way, she thinks the awful events of 1999 turned out to be one of the best things that could have happened to her. 'It took the pressure off. To go through your worst nightmare in public is oddly liberating, because now there is nothing more for me to be afraid of. And, if anything, it has made my relationship with Jonathan even stronger. We have talked about everything now. Nothing has been left unsaid. And, if we can cope with this, we can cope with anything.'

Jonathan was also willing to take his share of the blame for the pressure his wife had been put under. 'For most of our marriage, I have been swinging from one thing to another and I realise just how high-maintenance I was for Jane. Everything was about me, and my career. I was number one and the family had to fit in,' he said of the worst times. 'I was selfish, not because I saw my needs as being more important but because I just didn't stop and think about things. Now I do.'

Lessons had been learned on both sides; new foundations had been laid. It was time to move on – and there was a lot for the pair of them to do.

12

Number One on
Radio Two

Jonathan carried on with his Virgin Radio show throughout the early days of 1999 when the cracks first started to show in his personal life. He kept the jokes and the japes coming and listeners would only find out about his problems by reading the papers. Virgin bosses were the first to applaud his professionalism. But it turned out that they weren't the only ones paying attention to the way Jonathan's show was going. Over at Portland Place in central London, a group of BBC chiefs was also tuning in. They had recognised the fact that the cheeky chappie from Channel 4 had grown up – and they knew millions of his fans had grown up alongside him. So, of all places, they thought there could be an ideal slot for Jonathan on Radio Two.

Jonathan is the first to admit that, if he had been told in his twenties that he would one day end up on the middle-class, middle-aged bastion of Radio Two, then he would

dyed-in-the-wool station of yesteryear to the one with the fastest-growing audiences in the UK.

'Jonathan has the fastest mind to mouth of anybody I have ever worked with in my long career,' said James as the show's first anniversary approached and his recruitment was fully vindicated. 'His show has become an appointment to listen and challenges the audiences achieved in primetime television. Jonathan has a kind of renaissance feel about him – he is extremely gifted and all that is informed by a high intelligence.'

Lesley Douglas, who took over as station chief on James Moir's retirement, says that a lot of people were able to ride on Jonathan's wide coat tails. 'His appointment was absolutely key to the station. Just the fact that he wanted to work on it sent out fantastic signals.' Everyone else agreed. 'You just can't underestimate the Jonathan Ross effect,' said fellow broadcaster Stuart Maconie – a man whose own past on *NME* had made him even more concerned than Jonathan about taking a job on the station.

Throughout the troubles of 1999, Jonathan said walking into the Radio Two studios on a Saturday morning was always a refuge and a pleasure. He felt at home and in control there.

Perhaps surprisingly, the former punk fan who had once said he had the worst record collection in London turned out to have an instinctive feel for the sort of music he wanted to play and the sort his very mixed audience would like to hear. This subtle mix was vitally important to Radio Two's transition and survival. 'The changes to the station went by almost unnoticed because Radio Two's brand values have always remained constant. Our policy has always been to employ only genuine music fans. I think radio listeners were ready for something that was going to be intelligently and wittily presented. And music based, and challenging,' says Lesley Douglas.

Jonathan's nostalgia for the bands of his childhood chimed perfectly with the vast mass of 'generation X' listeners in his age group. But his ability to get interested in the latest performers – even while he took the mickey out of them – kept his show from being fossilised. It could have been a high-wire act, but he pulled it off.

What Jonathan liked about the station from the start was the sense that he was being trusted to run his own show on his own terms. The management had known what they were getting when they offered him the job, so they were prepared to let him get on with it. Jonathan's fellow presenters said the hands-off treatment brings out the best in everybody. 'There is an intimacy about the place that makes the whole station tick,' says Maconie, who now does shows on Radio Six and comes back to Radio Two to make occasional music documentaries. 'It sounds clichéd, but there is something very familial about it. It is relaxed; it isn't run by computers. It hasn't been focus-grouped. There is a lot of intuition in the building. What the station chiefs and all the presenters have done is to create the most successful radio station by saying there are no rules... by tearing up the rulebook and starting again.'

Steve Wright agreed – and more specifically said Jonathan fitted perfectly into that environment. 'Jonathan is one of the wittiest people in the business and he doesn't follow any of the rules.'

From his very first show, Jonathan made it abundantly clear that he was going to plough his own unique furrow on air. And the way the show was promoted certainly reflected it. 'Music, waffle and occasional insults,' was the best way that Radio Two marketing writers could think of describing the show in its promotional material.

For the vast majority of listeners, the waffle was what makes the show so successful. Sitting behind the mike in the subterranean studio, Jonathan lets his mind run riot as he rambles deliciously on. He talks about things he has read in the papers or seen on television, things that have happened to him, Jane and the kids in the week, things he remembers from years ago, stories other people have told him, people he has met, places he has been. Somehow, even the most trivial event can turn to comic gold when the 'On Air' lights are on – regular listeners say few weeks go by when they don't laugh out loud at one anecdote or another.

What makes Jonathan's humour work so well is the fact that he is so often prepared to be the butt of his own jokes. 'You're listening to someone falling apart before your very ears,' he said one week before his endlessly funny hypochondria triggered yet another lengthy discourse. One week, he also recounted the result of a health check he had gone though after worrying that he might be going deaf. 'The doctor said my hearing is fine... I just don't let anyone else get a word in edgeways,' he admitted. Jonathan's social, fashion or other gaffes are equally well painted. Utterly self-deprecating, he will detail in excruciatingly funny detail a crisis that had befallen him, an embarrassment, a humiliation or a miscalculation that others would prefer to keep secret. His problems become his listeners' punchlines, and the fact that so much of them were based on everyday experiences just intensified the humour. Because every listener had pushed a trolley round a supermarket, parked a car in a multi-storey car park or lost a dry-cleaning ticket, we can laugh even louder at the Mr Bean-style absurdity which ensues when Jonathan does the same. His life is every listener's life in surreal, boundary-stretching technicolour. And if we think we've got problems, hey, it could always be worse. We could slip on life's banana skins just like Jonathan seems to do each and every week.

That said, Jonathan was never going to be a faux 'Everyman' pretending to be humble when we all know he earns a fortune and lives the kind of life most of us can only dream of. So he was just as happy to show off about his latest holidays or trips. 'Where am I in the middle of next week? Oh yes, Hollywood, interviewing film stars. Flying First Class because I like all the space up there at the front of the plane. I want to be able to stretch out, enjoy myself when I'm travelling. All in the name of public service broadcasting,' he would crow, on air, to Andy.

Another gamble that paid off on the show was his decision to stay as wildly politically incorrect on air as he can be in real life. It felt natural and offered a huge breath of fresh air in otherwise troubled times. It doesn't matter if it is religion, race, sexuality, colour – Jonathan would tackle it head on. And, if female guests are getting fat, male guests are going bald – every taboo would be broken as he commented on it and mouthed off at his usual pace. The scatter-gun approach meant that, with so many people and issues in his sights, it was hard to take offence at any individual comment. 'Foreigners... Where would we be without foreigners? Everything about them is funny. The way they look, the way they speak, the food they eat, the things they do. They can't help it. Just being foreign is funny,' was one of the opening gambits to a story that summed it up. 'I can see your lips move and I know you are speaking but I can't understand a word you're saying,' he said when a Welsh guest with a strong accent came on the show.

What also brings the Saturday-morning show to life – it runs for a tough three hours every week – is the subtle soundtrack of a disbelieving or outraged Andy laughing in the background. Just as James Moir had predicted from the start, Andy was his friend's essential foil, and he says working with Jonathan is just as much fun as it sounds.

'We hardly ever discuss anything in advance of the show and it is certainly not scripted. Jonathan is funniest when he is being spontaneous and he is one of the funniest people I have ever met. I know I am famous for always laughing away in the background when Jonathan is telling one of his stories. But, as we have rarely discussed the stories before, I can't stop myself from laughing because I'm hearing it for the first time like everybody else,' he says.

The way the pair bounce thoughts and opinions (and insults) off each other has also become central to the relationship and the show. Andy is never too scared to try and rein his presenter in – although he rarely succeeds in doing it. 'Where are you going with this?' he asks, smiling behind his mike as another of Jonathan's anecdotes rambles on.

'Nowhere fast,' Jonathan replies, carrying on regardless.

What Jonathan also loved to do on air was to poke fun at all his Radio Two colleagues. Steve Wright, whose 'Seventies porn star' moustache is a constant topic in Jonathan's conversations, is a particular target. 'Stevie Wright... I saw him in the corridor the other day and I realised once again why he had to make a career out of radio,' being what seems like one in a million insults.

Not even Terry Wogan, the station's biggest name, is safe from the Ross riposte. 'Andy, you and I are the new jewel in the glittering Radio Two crown,' Jonathan boasted on air to his co-host after his, Terry's and Steve's shows were commended in an awards ceremony. 'Terry Wogan is now just the setting. Steve Wright is the kind of inner lining of the hat where the greasy hair goes.'

The photo call after the awards was also in line for a few digs. When the whole Radio Two team lined up for pictures, Jonathan claimed to be appalled. 'It was a sea of wrinkles. Some of them, you couldn't see their eyes without lifting up bits of their skin,' he said. And the jokes and descriptions kept on coming as the station continued to promote its winning team of presenters with other group photographs and commercials. 'You put us all together like that and it's frightening,' he said during one show after looking at the latest image. 'It's like the worst dysfunctional family in the world. You've got Jimmy Young, the granddad, pretending to be down with the kids; scary old Steve Wright, the moustachioed uncle; I'm the creepy mad uncle who no one knows what he gets up to; Mark Lamarr is the illegitimate son; Terry Wogan, the avuncular dad; Sarah Kennedy, the scary aunt that comes around and you tell the youngsters not to put the aftershave on or you might attract scary Aunt Sarah's attention. What a bunch.'

From the start, Jonathan's show was designed as a mix of chat, music and high-profile interviews – the radio equivalent of many of his favourite television formats. Just like on television, the selection of the guests was vitally important. Behind the scenes, this meant Jonathan did have a tough job trying to work out who to invite and what to say to them.

It was here that his show gained even more notoriety. The idealist in Jonathan didn't like the so-called 'selling celebrities' – the stars who went on every show in town as they tried to promote their latest book, film, album or other project. So, while the realist in him knew that he couldn't avoid these people, he decided at least to try to push them off balance during his chats. And he would fight to get others on the show as well. Some weeks, this included less well-known names that he felt deserved a wider audience. Other weeks, it meant big-name stars who had nothing to sell and so required a lot of wooing.

Neither type of guest was guaranteed a comfortable ride. Jonathan famously gave his old friend Steve Coogan a hard time on air when news broke about the comedian's extra-marital activities. He said that, when he first met *Little Britain* star Matt Lucas, he thought the man was a child with leukaemia on a 'meet-a-celebrity'-style visit fresh from his hospital bed. 'He looks like the kind of person who would never get adopted,' was another of his typical put-downs for an unphotogenic guest. And, in taboo-busting form, he was happy to emphasise failings more polite interviewers would ignore.

'So, you're 32 and still not a household name,' he began when interviewing one hitherto hopeful stand-up comedian. 'Thank you to you and your funny-looking friends,' he said after The Proclaimers had been on the show as part of their comeback trail.

Big stars were far from immune from his barbs and his jokes. 'I'd like to give you a pie. I'd like to give you a pie right now,' he said, with typical sideways suggestiveness to Victoria Beckham in the midst of her latest 'is she or isn't she an anorexic' battle with the press. By contrast, Jonathan also caused a mini-storm on the show when he told Dannii Minogue that she was looking fat – without making it clear that in his eyes this was a huge compliment.

George Michael – and his facial hair – was a frequent target. 'He looks like a seven-year-old who's gone to a birthday party dressed up as Desperate Dan and his beard looks like it has been painted on by an adult. Memo to George – Dear George, You look ridiculous.'

When two old-school guitarists came on the show, Pink Floyd's 60-year-old David Gilmour and Roxy Music's 55-year-old Phil Manzanera, Jonathan was on top form. 'They're two quite elderly men,' he fussed on air with Andy just before the guests arrived. 'Is it warm enough in here for them? Should we get blankets? Some warm sweet tea?'

Later that same show, Jonathan found out that his next guest, property television star Sarah Beeny, had just had a baby. 'Oh, fingers crossed she might breastfeed,' he said lasciviously, amidst a chorus of typical disapproval from Andy.

And Andy, of course, was far from immune to Jonathan's insults either. 'Don't worry, there will always be a job for you here at the BBC,' Jonathan told his sidekick after a redundancy plan at the corporation was announced in the media. 'Big buildings like this one don't clean themselves. Clocks will always need setting.'

Of course, over the years, some things did go wrong on the weekly show and Jonathan did frequently push the boundaries just a little too far. 'So, you're still with us then?' might not have been the most sensitive opening question for the drug-and-drink-loving Ozzy Osbourne, especially so soon after he had nearly died in a quad-bike accident. That time, Jonathan got away with it.

'Who died and made Rachel Hunter a model? If I drag up, I look more attractive,' was a less successful comment. And saying Toyah Willcox looked so awful that she shouldn't be allowed to appear on television any more was certainly seen as a step too far – especially for a distraught Toyah. 'He said I should go away and do something about it,' the singer remembers, saying she was devastated to hear the comments she felt were 'little more than body fascism'. In her book, *Diary of a Facelift*, she explains how the words ultimately helped push her towards the plastic surgeons.

Despite occasional lapses like this, most people agreed that Jonathan's humour was essentially benign. He seemed genuinely to enjoy his guests' company, even as he sent them up. In the process, he could go too far, however. He faced a wave of complaints after interviewing the seemingly innocuous *Bargain Hunt* presenter David Dickinson. Though, of course, it wasn't David himself who caused the crisis – it was Jonathan's comment on the new *Bargain Hunt* DVD: 'If you wait until the end, there is a scene with David bringing himself off on an ottoman.'

Radio Two, it seemed, was not quite ready for that one.

Warning bells also rang whenever Jonathan's interviews or ramblings strayed on to the subject of drugs. He himself has always been fiercely anti-drugs, but that didn't seem to stop him joking about them. He told actor Ralph Fiennes that opium would be a 'good retirement drug'.

'Doesn't it fry your brains?' Fiennes asked.

'Oh, who cares when you're that age,' Wossie countered, only to find that the broadcasting watchdogs did. They also cared when he joked about giving the date-rape drug Rohypnol to actress Helen Mirren.

'Think about that. And then email or ring us to complain,' he said after yet another near-the-knuckle comment which he rightly guessed would have taken some listeners' breath away. And many would take him at his word. Among many other comments and rulings, the industry regulator, the Broadcasting Standards Commission, rapped Jonathan over the knuckles the first time he used the word 'wanker' on Radio Two and said it was 'concerned' that a joke about the terminally ill had been 'unnecessarily callous'. After five years of broadcasting, Jonathan was said to have attracted more BSC interventions than any other presenter. When he told a colleague that a hand injury made him look like 'a slightly challenged youth like you would get on a Variety bus', he racked up yet another reproof. 'He exceeded the acceptable boundaries for transmission,' the watchdog decided. And outsiders were quick to add their own comments. Then Tory Culture Spokesman John Whittingdale said, 'While I do think that Jonathan Ross is very talented, I would hope his producers tell him he cannot keep provoking this kind of censure.'

Unfortunately for them, it wasn't easy for Jonathan's producers to get this message across, because they were drowned out by so many other voices saying how good the show had become.

The Sony Radio Academy Awards, announced each year at London's Grosvenor House hotel, are the longest standing and most prestigious in the industry. Seen as the 'Oscars' of radio for nearly a quarter of a century, they are the accolades that performers and producers are all desperate to win. But competition is increasingly tough. Output from some 260 commercial stations, nearly 60 local and national BBC stations and nearly 50 digital stations goes under the Sony microscope before an extensive shortlist of 1,200 best-in-category names are pulled together for final examination. More than 100 judges, including journalists, presenters, producers and radio-lovers then decide who gets the Bronze, Silver and Gold awards.

Jonathan won his first award, a Bronze in the Entertainment category, in 2001. He has won a top-three award every year since then and got his first Gold in 2003. Reading through what the judging panels have said of him over the years shows just how well thought of he is in the industry. 'Jonathan Ross is a seasoned broadcaster with effortless charm and one of the best storytellers in the business. The result is a show that's easy to enjoy,' they said in his first winning year. 'A raconteur "par excellence" – his appeal lies in saying things that his audience identifies with but would never articulate out loud. A really entertaining listening experience, verging on the outrageous,' they said the following year when he was upgraded to a Silver award.

'All the judges laughed out loud and Jonathan is one of the best TV and radio presenters we have,' they said when they gave him the Gold for Weekly Music Show of the Year in 2003. 'Witty, quick, intelligent and hugely entertaining, Jonathan's formidable and engaging personality dominates the show, but he is also a passionate music fan. The playlist is uniquely diverse for mainstream radio – ranging from forgotten classics to the latest artists, often performing live,' they said the following year, while, in 2005, when he got his second Silver in the Entertainment category, there was a light-hearted but still complimentary mention from the panel. 'This entry demonstrated a stylish, funny and gifted approach to live radio,' ran the commentary. 'The judges can't tell whether Jonathan Ross works really hard on his show, and hides it brilliantly, or whether he just turns up and does it all off the cuff.'

Collecting his award and wanting to hold on to some long-held tricks of the trade, Jonathan was happy to admit that it was a bit of both.

13
Beyond Compère

While radio had given Jonathan a second chance after the fallow years of his career, he owed an equal debt to a different genre – the awards show. Today, he is the ultimate show host, the suave, irreverent, brightly suited and utterly well-prepared master of any number of ceremonies. He is the universally accepted number-one choice for the big awards presentations that can take up three hours of primetime television. And, far from the public eye, he hosts a seemingly endless series of invitation-only corporate gigs, offering his trademark near-the-knuckle commentary and inescapable star power in return for one of the highest fees in the business.

'With Jonathan Ross, you get professionalism from the start,' says Natasha Stevenson, who books big-name speakers for a variety of corporate events. 'He wants to know exactly who the client is; he wants and clearly reads

197

all the information about them so he can talk knowledgeably about them at the event, and he doesn't come back with any ridiculous demands for the event itself. He turns up on time, is utterly charming and totally engaged; he gets the job done and then he leaves. That may not sound like particularly radical behaviour, but in the entertainment industry, when some celebrities really do want freshly decorated dressing rooms, special diets and "no eye contact" clauses in their contracts, Jonathan's attitude is refreshing to say the least.'

One of the other reasons why Jonathan, to this day, is so committed to offering value for money at corporate events is because they were where he cut his teeth in the industry. Back in the early days of *The Last Resort*, he was considered too new, too untested for any televised ceremonies, so the company gigs were all he was offered. And the man who had been too shy to stand up in class at school got to like the edginess of speaking in front of large groups of strangers at conferences and product launches. He even liked being heckled because it taught him to speed up his own reactions to events. It was a skill he would certainly need in the future when he one day shared awards stages with the likes of Julian Clary.

In the meantime, other equally unpredictable co-hosts would cause problems of their own. In one of his first high-profile attempts at being a master of ceremonies, he hosted the *TV Golden Break Awards* for ITV in 1990, for example. Filmed at the London Palladium, a 'stunt squirrel' called Cyril was an unofficial star of the show (he was standing in for the unknown grey squirrel that did the tricks in the hit Carling Black Label lager commercials). For a while, Cyril was happy to perch on Jonathan's shoulder. But, when he saw Pippin, a dog brought along by comedienne Helen Lederer, he jumped down, shot across the Palladium's stage and disappeared. 'I think Pippin has eaten Cyril,' Jonathan joked, before ITV executives came on stage and asked him to refilm the segment without the comment in case it upset young viewers.

A year later, Jonathan's peers in the entertainment world got another glimpse of his ability to control a room. It was 1991 and he was hosting the *British Comedy Awards*, being broadcast live on ITV to several million members of the public as well. As showcases go, it was hard to beat. But Jonathan was the first to admit that there were some big teething problems to address. He had written much of the script for that first ceremony with old friend Danny Baker – and soon came to regret it. 'On the night, everyone was drunk and I could hear him in the audience telling people on his table, "Oh, there's a good gag coming up now" or "Wait 'til you hear the punchline for this one." It wasn't easy to focus.'

Perhaps he wasn't quite as adept early on at carrying on regardless as he has become in later years. Jonathan's initial reviews as an awards host were negative to the point of hostility. Critics said he came over as too big for his boots, too irreverent, too amateur and too focused on the cliques of the broadcasting community to attract mainstream viewers at home. Many of his gags worked in the room, but were lost in translation when they were shown on television. And wasn't he just too damned young to take on such an important role?

For all his frivolity, Jonathan has always taken criticism to heart. It doesn't depress him as much as it used to, but it always preys on his mind and blackens his mood. So he tries to shake it off by treating the comments as constructively as possible and trying to learn from them. So, while he knew some of the attacks in 1991 could be dismissed as sour grapes, he felt others could help him out. He vowed to grow into the compère's role and he was over the moon when ITV said it wanted him in charge again the second year and the year after that.

By then, Jonathan's command of his stage had become almost complete. Far from having simply shaken off his childhood shyness, he was positively embracing the chance to be the centre of attention. That increased confidence has shown through in ever better performances on the awards stage – he has now hosted the *British Comedy Awards* for 16 consecutive years. Even when the BBC gave him a massive and exclusive contract in 2000, he demanded that they insert a get-out clause so he could have his annual ITV outing handing out the comedy gongs.

Over the years, Jonathan has subtly changed the way the show is structured – as usual taking his cues from the big American ceremonies he loves. So he has a longer, funnier introduction and plenty of banter with almost all of the guest presenters. In the process, he admits he can, as usual, overstep a few marks.

'I just can't help speaking my mind. I know I am probably cruising for a bruising and one day I am going to end up bumping into some celebs that I have bad-mouthed. I don't mean to be rude or unpleasant. I just get a little garrulous sometimes and forget the boundaries in the quest for a laugh,' he said of his awards introductions.

The *EastEnders* star Ross Kemp was one example. At one ceremony, Jonathan said Kemp was fancied by both men and women, 'despite the fact that he looks like an elephant's scrotum'. It didn't go down very well. 'I thought it was a funny line, but he didn't,' Jonathan says. 'When I next bumped into him, he said, "Last time you were on stage, you called me an elephant's testicle." After he had got it off his chest, he was very nice about it, but, one of these days, I am going to meet someone I have been genuinely rude about and I am going to pay for it.'

In the meantime, though, audiences always get to have a great laugh – and some commentators say Jonathan has single-handedly seen British comedy through many of its less successful years. 'It is ironic that, at the moment, the man presiding over the awards is invariably funnier than most of the people receiving them,' one commentator said in 2000. 'He is the sole reason for tuning into awards ceremonies... especially now that Caroline Aherne has sobered up.'

Jonathan managed to look so good for one simple reason – he put plenty of work into it. He was far from just a vacant anchorman reading other people's lines from an autocue and losing the plot when things failed to go to plan. Instead, he ruled the room, picking up on its mood and putting down its worst hecklers. 'Spending two and a half hours on your feet is murder on your back,' he joked when asked about the job. But it was also murder on your nerves, especially when the people who come on stage to collect or hand out awards can be drunk, drugged up or otherwise incapable of rational behaviour. Jonathan always steps back to let others take the limelight as the guest presenters arrive, but he is always ready to step back to the podium to shut them up or carefully bundle them off stage when required. What he likes about live ceremonies, he says, is that they take him back to the chaos and confusion he felt back in the early days of *The Last Resort*; the times when he had no idea how television was really made or what he should be doing, but when he had a feeling that audiences didn't really mind. Bad television can be great television if it's done with a knowing grin, was how he described it back then. And the knowing grin was almost always on his face on the awards podium. So it didn't matter how amateur it looked when microphones failed, satellite links broke or video clips stalled. The more technical hitches there were, the more human Jonathan looked; and the worse his fellow professionals behaved, the more viewers seemed to warm to the man charged with controlling them.

This was infamously illustrated in 1993 when Julian Clary was one of the show guests. At first, there was no indication that the night was to cause such controversy. As usual, Jonathan had worked on his script with his longstanding friend and collaborator Jez Stevenson. He had rehearsed the evening fully with longstanding awards producer Michael Hurll. And in the vast, subterranean London Studios, he had managed to insult and annoy everyone from Jerry Hall to wrestler Hulk Hogan within the first half-hour of the show. The atmosphere in the studio, he admitted afterwards, had felt more drunken and belligerent than in the past. Speeches from the likes of Michael Barrymore, Chris Evans and Danny Baker had gone well over their target length, so Jonathan knew he would have his work cut out to see all 22 awards handed out before the show's fixed end time. The pressure was on... and Julian Clary was about to go even further off-message.

'Good to see you. How's it hanging?' Jonathan greeted him, with no idea of the horror ahead.

'Oh, very well thank you. Very nice of you to recreate Hampstead Heath for me here,' Julian began, looking around at the strangely jungle-like set. 'As a matter of fact, I've just been fisting Norman Lamont.'

The entire audience was entirely silent for about a second of pure shock. Had they really heard what they thought they had heard? And did it mean what they thought it did? Then the laughter began and didn't stop.

'Let me ask you, Julian...' Jonathan tried desperately to interrupt and return to his script. But he had to admit he had been beaten and he tailed off into silence. Julian made another, even coarser comment, and Jonathan, seemingly the only person in the room to remember that the event was being broadcast live, tried again to rein his guest in. He failed.

'Are we still on?' he asked, ultimately, looking directly at the cameras. 'At least tonight has given schoolchildren a whole new expression to talk about in the playground tomorrow morning,' he said later, when Michael Barrymore raised the subject again after collecting his award for Best Entertainment Series.

The comments were to make fundamental changes to the way events like this were shown in the future. Live broadcasts were deemed simply too dangerous. If the whole package couldn't be pre-recorded, then time-delays would be introduced to ensure that the boundaries of good taste were not overstepped again. Julian Clary himself was cast into the television wilderness for almost a decade as the press furore about the night raged. But Jonathan found himself being widely praised. 'The 1993 awards remain a sparkling example of both astonishingly bad, yet also gruesomely addictive television and are therefore one of the best events of its kind,' says critic Ian Jones. 'Jonathan Ross's handing of this particular coverage stands as maybe the model example of matching sequential mishaps and mismanagements with exactly the right responses and rationale.'

It was a tragedy, Jones says, that Jonathan had proved himself so good on live television in an evening which ensured that 'live' would never actually mean the same thing again.

Over the ensuing years, Jonathan would dice with his own clever brand of danger, however. As his opening speeches got longer, he got better at both schmoozing and craftily abusing his audiences. 'So much Botox and fake tans, it's like I'm looking at the terracotta army,' he said looking out at the crowd in 2005. And he was always ready to lay into the worst shows of the previous year.

'Let's talk about *Celebrity Love Island*. Paul Danan, Rebecca Loos, Michael Greco on a coral atoll... Where's nuclear testing when you need it?' he asked to huge applause after that particular debacle.

Even awards winners can't escape his tongue. 'Remember phone-in polls are nothing more than mere popularity contests,' he said archly, as the first of them were introduced in the early 1990s. More than a decade on, he was still at it. 'Remember, this doesn't mean you're the best. It just means it's your turn,' he told the winners in 2005.

Comments like this punctured the chummy, cliquey, self-congratulatory balloon of television awards, and made viewers at home feel far closer to them. And they are one reason why Jonathan ensured that the ITV *Comedy Awards* has overcome the endemic 'awards fatigue' that has slashed audiences for almost all the other big industry bashes.

Bored with the Brits, baffled with the Baftas – that's how it seemed to be in 2006 when the latest figures came in. Despite a gold-plated celebrity audience, the most recent Baftas got a record low audience of just 3 million, part of a downward trend that saw 2004's 5.7 million viewers fall to 4.4 million in 2005. The Brits endured the same slump – more than a million fewer viewers were watching at the end of 2006's two-and-a-half-hour show as there were at the start. And the overall average, at 4.5 million, had fallen by 1.5 million in a year.

Jonathan's *Comedy Awards* still reigned supreme, though. The most recent show got more, rather than less, viewers than the one before. At a near record 5.4 million viewers, it beat the BBC's perennially popular *Sports Personality of the Year* show as well as the Baftas, Brits and all the other celebrity-focused televised ceremonies.

What added a little extra fizz to the role as the years went by was the fact that Jonathan was increasingly winning gongs as well as overseeing their distribution. The fact that his own shows were often competing in his much-derided telephone and text votes allowed for plenty of jokes throughout the evenings. So, win or lose, there were plenty of quips. 'It's good I lost. It makes me seem more human, less God-like,' he said after missing out to Ant and Dec in 2005, having made endless jokes at their expense all evening. Occasionally, however, Jonathan did do a Clary and get carried away by enthusiasm when he accepted awards. Winning the first major trophy for his radio show in 2000, he said he wanted to offer special thanks because 'I've only ever won a best-dressed award from the Spastics Society until now – and that was because I managed to do all my buttons up the right way.'

It turned out to be a massive miscalculation. The whole audience booed him – including, with some of the loudest hisses, his wife Jane. In his serious moments, Jonathan admits that this was one of the few comments he is genuinely ashamed of and one he has never really forgotten.

Proving himself at the big set-piece awards shows didn't just help pay Jonathan's huge mortgages in the fallow years of his career and provide a great extra gig when times were good. They also worked as a fantastic show-reel for other jobs. Broadcasters realised that

Jonathan's viewer-friendly style was perfect for major events – so he has since become a fixture on New Year's Eve and other special shows. Live commentary, over an extended period, is a lot harder than it appears, and the born-again talkaholic in Jonathan loved the challenge of filling hour after hour of screen time. His childhood love of trivia was always a huge help – if he didn't know some obscure facts about what might be going on around him, then he was always ready to try to imagine something. Always opinionated and always interested, he could fill gaps in schedules that would defeat most other commentators – and, if things went really wrong on a live broadcast, he could turn it into a triumph by drawing attention to it and laughing along with the viewers rather than pretending all was well. In all of this, his reputation for a quick wit preceded him – and helped him turn almost any circumstance to his advantage. 'Right from the start, I have been given the benefit of the doubt. Whatever I do, people assume I do it knowingly,' he admitted – saying that, in reality, he was often acting on adrenalin-fuelled instincts rather than any pre-formed plan.

The ability to keep shows going, no matter what, had been particularly well honed on some of Jonathan's earliest charitable broadcasts. He first got involved in Comic Relief and Red Nose Day back in his first heady days of fame on *The Last Resort*. Both were intensely personal projects which he stuck to throughout his wilderness years and which he continues to drive forward today. The first incarnation of Comic Relief came as part of Noel Edmonds's *Live Live Christmas Breakfast Show* on Christmas Day in 1985 amidst the African famine. A live BBC1 broadcast from a refugee camp in Sudan made it painfully clear how important a new fundraising effort would be, and comedians, of all people, were first in line to create one.

That first Christmastime broadcast called for emergency donations and was modestly successful. But the people behind it thought more could be done. Would a full-scale American-style telethon be worth considering? After a while, it was decided that it would be, as long as the evening could have a suitable theme to pull it together and give it some momentum for the future. That was where comedy came in – and when Red Nose Day was born.

Jonathan was one of the three presenters on screen for the first Red Nose Day in March 1988. Standing alongside Lenny Henry and Griff Rhys Jones, he held together the unique line-up of performers, whose jokes were interspersed with utterly shocking images of the poverty that still existed across huge parts of Africa. The whole evening was a gamble for everyone from the director general of the BBC downwards. If the pessimists were proved right, viewers would turn off and donations wouldn't come in. The presenters and the stars were ready for personal humiliation. But they were desperate that the charities they hoped to support wouldn't suffer, and, as it turned out, they didn't. More than £15 million was raised that first night. With ever bigger events taking place every two years since then, Red Nose Day has become an essential part of the country's fundraising efforts.

More than £400 million has now been raised and distributed to charities and projects at home and overseas. In Britain, Red Nose Day money has funded work with young people, pensioners, the mentally ill and victims of domestic violence. Overseas, it has helped health and educational efforts, as well as the original famine relief. Jonathan himself was one of the key drivers behind the Red Nose juggernaut's educational and awareness drives. He believed that giving money was only one part of the equation, and that people would accept information as well as entertainment. And so the serious side of the Comic Relief events share top billing with the jokers.

That said, of course, Jonathan was also prepared to do whatever it took to get people laughing while they handed over their credit card details. If that meant anything from a marathon snog with the Spice Girls at the height of their fame in 1997 to the bizarre hairstyles of 2003 and 2005, then he was always ready to pitch in. Over the years, Jonathan has become one of the 'voices' of the show, as well as one of its biggest faces. He does the voice-overs for many of the preview trailers, as well as hosting the spin-off Comic Aid concert at London's Hammersmith Apollo in 2005. Other big live events for different causes include his role holding Bob Geldof's Live8 concert together in 2005. Wearing a suit Ricky Gervais said was 'the colour of baby diarrhoea', Jonathan was in typically irreverent form. 'I hope he's got a ticket,' he said as United Nations Secretary General Kofi Annan took the stage to make a speech. In his interviews and commentary, everyone from Elton John, Madonna and U2 all came in for the usual barrage of insults or 'Ross rockets' as the *Daily Express* called them the following day.

Behind the scenes, Jonathan is also one of the big guns the Red Nose Day charity can call upon when it needs to twist a few arms in the corporate world. The trustees negotiate deals with government, companies and individuals so that all the running costs of the charity are covered – meaning every penny in every pound donated by the public can go to good causes. Over the years, Jonathan has taken up several other charities, though much of his work is done out of the public eye. He is a trustee, for example, of the little-known Lowe Syndrome Trust, which funds research into the rare genetic disease that hits young boys, for example.

When Jonathan does break cover on the good-works front, he is prepared to annoy some of his core city-dweller fans – as he did when he backed the anti-piracy campaigns for DVDs and videos. He took on the campaign, not because of pressure from the film industry worried about shrinking corporate profits, but because of the conversations he had with police and victim-support groups about how the proceeds of the illegal industry tend to be spent. Buying a cheap pre-release DVD in the pub or shopping centre might seem like an economic and painless activity that harms no one. It isn't. 'It's not a victimless crime, it feeds everything from human trafficking, money laundering, drugs, benefit fraud and violence. Saying "yes" to a pirate DVD is saying "yes" to crime on your street,' Jonathan argues, repeating the message whenever he can, in spite of the cynicism of some of his fans.

One final piece of charity work Jonathan agreed to went badly wrong, however. He and Jane appeared on the celebrity-couples version of *Who Wants to Be a Millionaire* and were on £16,000 when the question came up asking how many episodes of *Coronation Street* had been broadcast to date. The correct answer was 5,000, but the Rosses got it wrong – and their charity saw its payment slump to just £1,000. Mortified, the couple did then make up the difference with a private cheque later. But they've never done a game show together since.

14

Chat Wars

'Look, it's going yellow!' And with those four words, Jonathan stood up, unzipped his trousers and flashed a key part of his anatomy at Gordon Ramsay, the rest of the *They Think It's All Over* regulars and the stunned 400-strong studio audience at the BBC TV Centre in Wood Lane, west London.

It was December 2000 and Jonathan was in his usual seat as the BBC's sports quiz was being recorded. He had been drafted into the show's regular line-up when comedian Lee Hurst stepped aside as a regular panellist – and, while he was no big sports fan, Jonathan's laddish, *Loaded*-style sense of humour meant that he fitted in from the start. 'We get a pretty free hand at the Beeb now,' he said of the way the show is made. 'We get away with a lot of stuff that you couldn't have done even a couple of series back. It's ruder, more ribald, more robust, and all those other words I can't pronounce.'

But was the show really ready for a Full Monty from one of its regulars? Jonathan gave it a try after making the headlines for being hit in the groin while clay pigeon shooting the previous week. Someone asked how he was. 'It's done me permanent damage,' he said – before dropping his trousers to prove it. The audience went wild – and so did Jonathan's fellow celebrities.

'I am thinking of getting the shot of Ian Wright recoiling in perhaps too much horror printed up on a T-shirt. It was like he had never seen a grown man naked before. Nick Hancock's expression was even better. It went from terror to shock to intrigue and then to envy. David Gower is very jealous because he missed it. He's been begging me for a private showing ever since,' Jonathan joked after watching the pre-edited version of the show (clever cuts meant that nothing too embarrassing was on display when the show was finally broadcast – though that didn't stop sales of the DVD version of the show beating all previous records when that series was finally released). Of course, the scene, and the inevitable furore, really only increased Jonathan's appeal and his currency on the show.

He had taken on the role – for an estimated £100,000 a year – as part of a huge new BBC contract he had signed in the summer of 2000. At that time, Jonathan had been on a roll with his radio show and the BBC had been in trouble. Ant and Dec had just defected to ITV, following in the well-paid footsteps of Des Lynam and Frank Skinner. The BBC was determined that Jonathan would not follow suit – and, while it was happy for him to continue with his annual *Comedy Awards* outing on ITV, it offered him a long-term £2.5 million golden-handcuffs deal to ensure all his other shows would stay on the Beeb.

The exact details of the contract were not revealed at the time. But it is now known to include some fascinating features. One was a big pay boost for his film show, by then well into its second year and widely seen as a hit. When he had first signed up to *Film '99*, Jonathan had been prepared to 'loss lead' and was working for less per show than on anything he had done since the late 1980s. Now he was being upgraded to a £250,000-a-year deal, due to run until at least 2003. Similar amounts were already coming into his bank account for his Radio Two show and for *It's Only TV But I Like It*. The combined payments finally pushed Jonathan into the entertainment super-league, alongside the likes of Des Lynam, Chris Tarrant, Cilla Black and star-of-the-moment Carol Vorderman. 'I am delighted with my deal but I strongly suspect that the BBC has signed me mainly because I weigh as much as the recently departed Ant and Dec combined,' he said jokingly as news of the contract broke.

As it turned out, the money was particularly welcome that year because one of Jonathan's biggest get-rich-quick ventures had just crashed and burned. At the start of the year and on the crest of the dot-com wave, he had joined the likes of Oprah Winfrey, Cindy Crawford and David Beckham as the face of an internet-based company. Jonathan's company was toyzone.co.uk and the firm's founder, PR guru Matthew Freud, said he was perfect for the role. 'We chose our celebrity face very carefully.

Jonathan is exactly what Toyzone sets out to be – enthusiastic, irreverent, a bit of a child, but in an adult way.'

If all had gone well, the venture could have made him very rich, very quickly – this was, after all, the era when the founders of lastminute.com and Amazon had become multimillionaires almost overnight. Freud admitted that his client's contract was structured in pretty much the same potentially lucrative way. 'Jonathan is a participant in the business, rather than just a hired hand. He has a standard endorsement deal but with an equity figure at the end of the arrangement.' In plain English, that meant that, instead of earning a wage, Jonathan would be paid for the use of his image with a share in the company. The share itself was tiny – estimated at just 1 per cent of the business. But, when investment bank Lehman Brothers predicted that Toyzone could be worth £250 million within 12 months, Jonathan's stake suddenly looked like a very substantial asset. As it turned out, however, the dot-com bubble soon burst and, instead of taking over the retail world, Toyzone had all but disappeared less than a year after it was formed. So, instead of a £2.5 million payout, Jonathan was left with nothing. Still, nothing ventured, nothing gained, he thought, as his accountants dealt with the aftershock. And, anyway, the new BBC contract, coincidentally enough, was for almost exactly the same amount as he had been hoping to earn from his high-tech adventure. So he was hardly likely to be taking in washing to make ends meet in the near future.

As he and his agent examined the BBC contract, the final detail that made Jonathan happiest of all was the

So, while he was happy to talk about any forthcoming programmes, he always tried hard to steer questions away from his home life, his marriage, family or any of the other subjects he tries to keep off limits.

'It's great to be at the BBC...'

When the first show was finally broadcast, Jonathan was sitting behind his regulation desk in the centre of the set with an equally regulation smile on his face. Andy was to his left, his new house band, 4 Poofs and a Piano, were to his right and the next eight weeks of Friday nights stretched out in front of him. He and his four writers had put together a typically good introduction, as well as a decent review of the latest celebrity gossip. For viewers, there was one other clever surprise – there was a camera in the Green Room where the guests sat waiting to be introduced and to where they returned after the interviews. Jonathan had made it a requirement of the show that the guests did indeed sit there rather than waiting alone and unseen in their individual dressing rooms. Over the years, it would make for some great moments, not least when Martin Scorsese appeared on the show, clearly totally bemused by the unknown Brits sitting next to him. Being able to zoom back in on the guests whenever Jonathan wanted to crack a joke at their expense was another benefit.

In the first show, the Green Room was being shared by Johnny Lydon (one of Jonathan's childhood punk heroes), former *EastEnder* Tamzin Outhwaite (a pal of his mum's) and Neil Hannon from The Divine Comedy (a band he loved). So Jonathan could hardly complain about having to talk to people he didn't like or didn't find interesting. Not that this meant he was entirely happy with the show. Less than 12 hours after it had been broadcast, Jonathan and Andy were able to carry out a very public post-mortem on the Radio Two show. Once again, it was good publicity for the series, reminding listeners of what they had missed but could see again the following Friday. And, for all the pair's grumbles about bad editing or missed opportunities, they did seem broadly pleased with what they had achieved.

Viewers, though, looked like needing a little more time to get used to the show. The first episode attracted just 3 million viewers to BBC1, some 300,000 less than Graham Norton had got that same night over on Channel 4. On a 'paid per viewer' basis, this certainly didn't do Jonathan any favours. Television accountants had apparently worked out a way of proving whether stars were value for money – by dividing their salaries by the size of their audiences. Among the big chat-show hosts of the day, Frank Skinner fared worse – he cost 42 pence for every viewer attracted. Jonathan cost his employers 33 pence per viewer while Parkinson's huge audiences meant he offered a bargain-basement deal of just 4 pence per viewer. Despite the pseudo-accounting, it was desperately unscientific stuff. But it was just the kind of research that could turn into a self-fulfilling prophecy and push a fledgling show towards failure. So there would be some worried faces at Broadcasting House if Jonathan's ratings didn't pick up fast.

Fortunately, the critics were ready to call Jonathan's

new show a hit – even though Michael Parkinson said he remained unconvinced that it was what the public wanted. The on-off war of words between the two men and their various supporters was far from over. 'People prefer the more traditional talk shows to the new people like Jonathan Ross. The problem is they are over-contrived. He is a good comic but he tries to make himself the star of the show,' was Michael's latest salvo. But others said that it was Jonathan's very grandstanding that made his show work.

The *Sun*'s television critic Ally Ross said Jonathan could always trump Parky. 'Ross has got about five different gears and, when it doesn't work, he turns to comedy. Parky's got one gear and, if it doesn't work, he has to wind up the interview,' the critic concluded.

Fellow arts critic Mark Lawson was equally damning of the old-timer. 'What Parkinson has always said is that what he brought to the interview was his skill as a journalist, but the pickle he is in now is that he is not journalistic enough to ask all the tabloid questions,' he said.

Tabloid-obsessed Jonathan, of course, had no problem with any of that. And, as October turned to November, audience levels did pick up dramatically and the BBC confirmed that, after the initial run of eight shows, it was commissioning a longer run of 15 in the New Year. *Friday Night with Jonathan Ross* looked as if it was here to stay.

But, before the next run was to begin, Jonathan had something else to look forward to. Fulfilling a long-held dream, he had been asked to play a part in one of his favourite sitcoms. And, as a non-actor, he was hoping he would be up to the task because the part in question was for 'Jonathan Ross, quiz show host'. It would be a stretch, but he would see if he could make it fit, he told his agent with a smile when the call came through.

The show was the 2001 Christmas Day episode of *Only Fools and Horses*. 'As himself, Jonathan was a bit wooden, somewhat under-rehearsed but broadly convincing,' the critics said. The episode in question, the 64th of the extraordinary show, was entitled 'If They Could See Us Now'. It was set two years after Del and Rodney had finally become millionaires and left Peckham far behind. And, of course, everything had subsequently gone wrong. All the money had been lost in some dodgy investment schemes and everyone was back in Nelson Mandela House licking their wounds and trying to work out what to do next. Jonathan's role was as the host of *Goldrush*, a fictional quiz show that Del entered to try to win £100,000. He didn't, of course. For Jonathan, who was happy to send himself up in any way that *Only Fools'* writer John Sullivan wanted, the whole experience was magical. He said it was pretty much a dream come true to work even briefly with the likes of David Jason and Nicholas Lyndhurst and watch true sitcom magic come alive.

The sheer pleasure he got out of this one-off show encouraged Jonathan to take on similar ventures whenever his schedule allowed. People who criticise him for his ubiquity on television – and moan about how much he must be earning – are sometimes mistaken about his motives. Many of his unlikely appearances are done for rock-bottom prices, simply because Jonathan wants to take part in a show he admires.

So, over the years, he has appeared, pretty much as himself, on the likes of *The 10 Percenters* and *Jonathan Creek*, while he has been a guest on everything from *The Kumars at No 42*, *The Mrs Merton Show*, *French & Saunders*, *Bo' Selecta!* and *Top Gear*. And following on from the success of the *Only Fools and Horses* Christmas special came several specials of his more regular shows. In 2001, he also had a blast dressing up as a pantomime cow, complete with working udders, in *They Think It's All Over*, for example, alongside David Gower as a big-eared elf and Rory McGrath as Widow Twanky.

As 2002 got under way, there was plenty of more serious behind-the-scenes work to be done on *Friday Night with Jonathan Ross*, though. Several tweaks were to be made to the overall look and feel of the show before the second series was filmed, although Jonathan was determined to keep the overall tone as light-hearted as before. Sadly for everyone, one of the biggest changes saw Andy's on-screen role reduced and then finally deleted – it was felt that his interruptions and cues worked fantastically on radio but didn't seem to translate to the small screen. But Jonathan's desk, house band, on-camera Green Room and topical introductions all remained. And the sweet sense of danger every time Jonathan got a twinkle in his eye became palpable. Fans say that you can somehow tell when he is genuinely enjoying himself, that he is like a small child when he suddenly hits upon a particularly naughty or unlikely line of questioning... and that he is frequently egging himself on to break yet another chat-show taboo.

One of very many controversial examples of this arose when he had one of his favourite film stars on the show – Nicole Kidman. And, after a very short time talking about her latest work, he hit upon something else to discuss – women with read hair... and not just on their heads.

Kidman, appearing to be less comfortable with every passing second, tried several times to change the subject. But Jonathan was like a dog with a bone and, for all the anger it would cause, he wouldn't let go. 'I don't know whether just to end this now,' Kidman said at one point as her host went off on another taboo tangent. 'I hate doing these shows,' she was heard to say to production staff in the wings as Jonathan finally wrapped up.

So had Jonathan gone too far? The row, which intensified over the coming days, did suggest that he had. Kidman fans in particular were incensed at the way their heroine had been treated. 'I never like Ross at the best of times. He's a smarmy, self-centred git consistently trotting out crap, scripted jokes and sucking up to his guests and whatever film/book/album they are plugging, no matter what it is,' wrote one subscriber to a fansite. 'But his treatment of Kidman was simply appalling. From the outset, Ross made it clear that the main comedic thrust of the interview was going to be him lusting over her good looks. Kidman was clearly bored and frustrated with these cheap jokes, remarking, "You're repeating yourself," when he went back to the subject one more time. Ross also frequently got his research wrong with Kidman having to correct him and he frequently ignored Kidman's answers to his questions, sticking to the script and his lewd anecdotes instead.'

As the storm raged, the BBC was forced to bring out a statement on the matter in a bid to clear the air. 'Nicole Kidman was a wonderful guest with a great sense of humour who made a good interview even better with her responses,' the official response began. 'She didn't take offence at Jonathan's line of questioning and any regular viewers of *Friday Night with Jonathan Ross* will know that part of Jonathan's interviewing technique is a certain amount of innuendo. Nicole Kidman reacted superbly and this made for an extremely entertaining interview.'

Others said Jonathan's show, and those of rivals like Graham Norton and Frank Skinner, had turned into 'vehicles for smut' rather than chat and information. Pressure group Mediawatch UK was constantly demanding new constraints to be put on hosts such as Jonathan, who it saw as symptomatic of a deeper malaise in the television industry. 'There is a quest for controversy and producers and hosts seem to think it is their job to push the limits. Right across the schedule, there is a lot that fails to stand up to the test of good taste and decency,' said the group's director John Beyer.

As far as Jonathan was concerned, that didn't just apply to *Friday Night with Jonathan Ross* either; just as he was dealing with the fall-out from the Nicole Kidman interview, he got his knuckles wrapped after comments he made on *It's Only TV But I Like It*. A warning came through from the BBC governors after an episode involving a picture of Rolf Harris cradling a baby chimpanzee. 'And you'll be pleased to know they found a home for that lovely Romanian orphan,' Jonathan had joked, a line the producers were told to edit out of any repeats and DVD sales of the show.

By the time he made this remark, though, Jonathan had already decided that *It's Only TV But I Like It* had probably had its day. It was still performing well, if not spectacularly, in the ratings. But Jonathan couldn't help feeling that the world had moved on from taking the mickey out of television. The cast list reflected his thoughts. Julian Clary was still on the show, but Jack Dee had been replaced by Phill Jupitus as the other team captain, while the largely A-list team members of the first series had never really been replicated in subsequent years. As the show bowed out in 2002, the producers were only able to field a reserve team of guests. The Krankies, Coleen Nolan and a largely forgotten *EastEnders*' actor waved goodbye at the end of the final show. It had been good while it lasted, but everyone agreed that it was time to move on.

Back on Fridays, Jonathan was relishing the opportunity to occasionally mix up the standard format of the show and introduce some big set-piece interviews. *Friday Night with Jonathan Ross and Bowie* was one of them – with Jonathan on the edge of his interview chair as his hero performed three numbers live with his band. The same format for *Friday Night with Jonathan Ross and Madonna* was an even feistier show – and, as the sparks and the jokes flew, Jonathan felt he was finally able to answer the critics who had so savagely mocked the first interview he had done with the performer way back in his *Saturday Zoo* days.

He also felt that, with *Friday Night...*, he could answer other critics who said his off-message interview technique would scare off the big celebrity guests. Conventional wisdom had it that stars would only want to be on shows where they knew they would get a predictable easy ride from their interviewer. Jonathan thought differently and fans said his wild style won rather than lost him guests. 'When big names go on a traditional chat show, they have to perform well, be funny, interesting and entertaining and it can be a strain,' says pop columnist Gordon Collins. 'But they started to spot the fact that, when they go on *Friday Night with Jonathan Ross*, he will do all that for them. He'll crack the jokes so they don't have to. As long as the guests laugh along with the audience and agree to be lampooned a little, then they will come out of it looking good. In effect, they get a lot out of their appearances in return for very little input of their own and that's one reason why he does win the big names.'

And this was important, because, despite all the relaxed insouciance he tried to effect in public, winning the chat wars did matter to Jonathan. So he secretly loved the fact that he had indeed built up enough clout to win some of the world's most impressive, and often reclusive, guests.

In the autumn of 2004, for example, his chat-show coup was to get a rare audience with Paul Newman, though Parky then hit back by bagging a slot with Tom Cruise and, in 2006, it was Parky, perhaps unsurprisingly, who got Tony Blair on his show.

Still, with ratings of around 5 million a week, Jonathan could hardly complain about his Friday-night run. And he is the first to say that the whole team have a whole lot of fun in the production process. Most of the people who were behind the scenes when the series first began were largely still together several years later, even though some had taken a few sabbaticals and worked on other shows in the meantime. Many had done very well out of having *Friday Night...* on their CVs. His David Letterman-inspired house band, 4 Poofs and a Piano, for example, have won a huge number of lucrative corporate gigs on the back of their appearances. They have also released a single, taken their show *Never Mind the Botox* to the Edinburgh Festival and gone on a national tour in support of, of all people, Joan Collins. 'Not bad for, well, four poofs and a piano,' Jonathan says with a smile.

The men's success could perhaps have been anticipated, however, for over the years Jonathan has effectively turned his shows into finishing schools for people and acts who couldn't get a break anywhere else. Vic Reeves made his television debut on *The Last Resort*; Paul Whitehouse and Kathy Burke appeared first on the ill-fated *An Hour with Jonathan Ross* in the early 1990s; Caroline Aherne made her TV debut as Sister Mary Immaculate on *Tonight with Jonathan Ross*, while Mark Lamarr was the warm-up man; Jo Brand and Mark Thomas were all given a stage on *Saturday Zoo*. All are still close friends of the man who gave them their early shot at stardom – and former Channel 4 boss Michael Grade says one of the toughest tasks in television is to find anyone who speaks ill of Jonathan.

Back in 2002, with so much still ahead, the future should have been looking pretty rosy for Jonathan. *Film 2002* was on the cards, the longer series of *Friday Night with Jonathan Ross* was being filmed and his comedy panel shows were still making him, and their audiences, laugh. Jonathan was also about to take on a new semi-regular role, on the topical *Have I Got News for You* show (where he was first introduced as a man with 'the dress sense of a lobotomised pimp' and would be mocked, relentlessly, about his hair and clothes on almost every subsequent episode). That said, he did manage to more than hold his own alongside show regulars such as Paul Merton, Ian Hislop and Angus Deayton.

Back at home, the wider Ross family was also doing well – Paul was revelling in his younger brother's resurgent career. 'I do well now because producers are starting to say, "If we can't get Jonathan, we'll get a Ross who is older, uglier and shorter – but cheaper," and that works fine for me,' he would joke. Jane was going through a professional and personal renaissance as well. Her interest in the psychic world, the paranormal and the supernatural had intensified and, just as she had done with roller coasters, she had found a way to turn it into a career. In 2002, she was taking her first steps towards becoming a television presenter in her own right. So everything should have been perfect in the Ross household as spring turned to summer. But, as in the past, when silver clouds filled the sky, the grey linings were about to show.

15

A Cry For Help

It is hard to say exactly why the Ross marriage is so
fascinating to certain sections of the media, or why
some reporters seem so desperate to see it fail. But, in
2002, Jonathan and Jane lived with this constant pressure
on a daily basis and, often, they felt as if they couldn't do
right for doing wrong. If they weren't seen out in public
very often there were hints that they were estranged, or
even 'living separate lives', as one paper put it early that
year. If they did head out together, often in trademark
wildly complementary clothes, the same papers could
suggest that the pair were trying too hard to present a
united front, that their public displays of affection were
simply a mask to shield the fact that, yes, they were
estranged and living separate lives.

Over time, the couple had learned to live with the gossip
and innuendo, although sometimes the rumours did
become too loud and the claims too extravagant to ignore.

Reports that Jonathan had reached some sort of breaking point with his marriage and had moved out of the family home to stay with old friend Frank Skinner seemed too ludicrous to deny that same year. But, when no one did deny the reports, they appeared to gain even more credence. Locked in a catch-22 situation, the couple simply battened down the hatches and tried to get on with their lives. And, as every working parent with three growing children will attest, that means sometimes dealing with tensions, arguments and disagreements.

'Children are a boon to a relationship but, in many ways, they are the greatest strain as well,' Jonathan admits. 'So much time is taken up dealing with them, the emotional side of their development, the actual physical tending and caring for them, so that parents don't have time with each other that much. So, now we know this, Jane and I do try to remember it and make time for each other as well.'

For her part, Jane was the first to admit that the couple's relationship could be fiery. 'It's not like we have had no problems, because everybody now knows that we have,' she said. 'But we do work through things because you do have to work at relationships and, for us, it has always been worth it. We argue, but we don't have big rows where you upset each other dreadfully. We have short, shouty rows that clear the air.'

While the vultures in the tabloids couldn't seem to see it, this was actually a pretty healthy way to live. And it worked well for the Rosses – at least until the media pressures became just a little too much even for them to bear.

Things came to a head in the summer of 2002 when Jane was rebuilding her own career from beneath Jonathan's shadow. As part of that challenge, she had taken on a role in Channel 4's ingenious *Crime Team* show. The premise was that she and her colleagues would be presented with the facts of a grisly murder from a century or more ago, often one involving witchcraft, poisoning and intrigue. They then had to investigate it and try to find the culprits using only the forensic tools that were available at the time. A barrister, Jerome Lynch QC, was on hand to guide the investigation and a whole production team helped create the spooky atmosphere of the era in the various reconstructions.

The show Jane worked on that summer involved a three-day shoot in Otley, near Leeds, so Jonathan was holding the fort with the children in London while Jane was away. It was just the kind of relaxed, easy arrangement that countless working couples have when one partner has a work commitment away from home. But, as Jonathan and Jane would find, things are not so easy when you are in the public eye and the media is desperately trying to unearth juicy gossip about your relationship.

Jonathan and Jane spoke on the phone several times a day during the shoot and had particularly long conversations in the evenings, going over everything from their work to their children, again just as any other working couple might. Meanwhile, the newspapers ran their usual round of unbelievable stories.

Jane says her husband tends to be far more affected by lies or inaccuracies in the papers than she is. Jonathan reads more, thinks about it more and then worries more. And with a huge workload on his own shoulders – in 2002, he was making more shows than in any year since his first big break in 1987 – he was letting the pressure affect him more than he should.

With Jane still away with *Crime Team*, Jonathan realised that he, too, needed a break, a chance to let off steam with an old friend and unwind. Unfortunately for him, and fortunately for the gossip columnists, that old friend was both pretty and female. Keyboards were tapping in newspaper offices almost as soon as tongues started wagging. Jonathan and magazine writer Emily Dean headed into Hampstead for a coffee and a catch-up. They sat and talked for nearly an hour at a pavement table outside the north London café. It was far from a cloak-and-dagger assignation and, as this fact sank in, the gossip columnists were temporarily stumped. It was hard, even for them, to suggest cracks in the Ross marriage when this was all they had to go on.

They would soon get their story, however. On top of all the other pressures, Jonathan wasn't feeling well. He was furious and upset about the way the media were writing about Jane, and a part of him was furious at her for giving them even the smallest piece of ammunition for their phoney war. So, suddenly, he let go. As a paparazzi camera started to whirr, he began to cry. He put his head in his hands as the tears started to flow, trying to hide his distress from the people around him. Emily put her arm around her friend's shoulders to try to comfort him as they walked back to his car.

When the pictures were wired, though, the papers, needless to say, went wild. Full-page articles in the tabloids crowed about this supposed new threat to the Ross marriage, and picked at all the old wounds of their previous separation. Was this an affair for Jonathan? Something else entirely? It hardly mattered. The papers hinted at anything and everything and all the usual unnamed 'sources' and 'friends of the couple' were dragged up to give whatever comments were required to suit the story. One paper even launched a savage attack on Jane's parents – and said that she, in turn, was to blame for her husband's anguish. The same paper also repeated all the old false claims that Jane had suffered bulimia as a teenager.

It was open season on both her and Jonathan once more. So it was little wonder that the whole family felt they needed to get away. They had a wonderful weekend in the country while the latest media furore was at its peak, and booked flights for an extended break at their Florida house the following month. By the time the five of them walked through the doors of their Florida home, the family was happier than ever, with Jonathan and Jane strangely triumphant that they had survived yet another savage onslaught by the media. The five of them ultimately spent nearly a month swimming, fishing, riding bikes and relaxing in the autumn sunshine.

A few paparazzi did bother them occasionally that particular autumn. But, when it was clear that Jonathan and Jane were content, it seemed as if, in the cynical world of British newspapers, the value of any snatched photographs was just about zero. So, after a while, the photographers packed their bags and headed off in search of less happy families elsewhere.

Back in Britain, the Ross family had another secret world to disappear into after heading through Heathrow – where Jonathan almost lost his trademark smile when the immigration officer looked carefully at his passport photo and then told him he had put on weight. The family had first thought about moving out of their home on the edge of Hampstead Heath in 1999 in search of more space and privacy. But it had taken a while to find the perfect new property. Work commitments meant they didn't want to be too far out of London and nor did they want to take their children too far from their friends – all three were either at or about to start school and they didn't want that to be disrupted. So, after talking to a series of discreet estate agents, they settled upon Hampstead Garden Suburb, less than a couple of miles from their old home and a world away from the noise and stress of central London.

As a former social historian, Jonathan particularly loved the chance to learn more about his new neighbourhood and the extraordinary lives of the cosmetics heiress and the mining engineer who had helped found it in the early part of the 20th century. The idea back then was to create a calming, socially balanced environment for all age and income groups. Wide roads, decent gardens and plenty of trees were to be the defining features of the area – and, while today's residents still enjoy all those benefits, the social mix has certainly changed greatly. Hampstead Garden Suburb now has a reputation for housing some of the richest, but most private people in north London. The properties are big, but often set well back from the road and totally anonymous. So, in many ways, it was the perfect location for a 40-something Radio Two DJ and his family. Gone were the couple's Brit-pop, reality-television and film-star neighbours of mainstream Hampstead. Now they would be rubbing shoulders at the local deli with the likes of King Constantine of Greece, while Richard and Judy's front door was no more than a couple of lawn tennis court lengths away from their own.

The new seven-bedroom house cost a staggering £2.6 million, an amazing purchase for a boy brought up in a three-bed council house in Leytonstone. Four decades after sharing a bedroom with four of his brothers, Jonathan could clearly afford to give his own children a quite different start in life. The new house is built on land once owned by Eton College and has an acre of gardens in which there is a tennis court, aviary, ornamental pond and indoor swimming pool. The three Ross children share a playroom, music room, private bathrooms and a games room – and their bedrooms were designed exactly the way they wanted them. Betty, for example, had become a big nature lover, so her room had bright-green grass-like carpet, curtain rails like branches and bedposts that looked like logs. Harvey's bed looked like a pirate ship and had been built by designer and family friend Lee Brown. His room also had a huge colourful mural Jonathan and Jane had painted based on scenes from a favourite computer game. Finally, Honey's room was what her mother described as 'Barbara Cartland pink' and stuffed with soft toys and dolls.

Adult guests can enjoy the Jacuzzi, snooker room and high-tech entertainment room, where Jonathan's vast DVD collection dominates proceedings. 'They're everywhere,' he said of his film collection. 'Sit down and you might find a video or DVD stuck up your jacksie when you get up.'

The equally film-mad Jane admits she hardly helps the situation either. She is almost as obsessive about Russ Meyer and Japanese horror films as her husband is, and admits her share of their joint DVD collection 'threatens to engulf the house' on a regular basis.

As before, both Jonathan and Jane have their own offices in the house – his has padded walls and ceilings and is based on a set in an *Avengers* film he had seen as a teenager and never forgotten. Once a week, he spends up to nine solid hours sitting in the office watching films for his review show, so he felt he could justify making a dream come true when considering its decor. He writes most of his scripts there as well, has a huge film reference library there and has started to hold more and more meetings at home, having long since lost the thrill of hanging out in Soho screening rooms or advertising agencies.

In the private and well-protected gardens, there are separate staff quarters, set in a self-contained unit that is nearly three times the size of Jonathan's first flat in Shepherd's Bush – yet another clear indication of how far he has travelled. Back inside the main house, the emphasis is on family, with photos on most surfaces and toys on most floors. But there are some typically unique features as well. Jane says she is endlessly looking through interior design magazines and clipping out articles that inspire her. So the whole house is full of great details, unique possessions and a fair few surprises.

For a start, there is the sheer number of televisions – at last count, Jonathan says the house has more than ten. Visitors may also notice that there seem to be crates of Evian water bottles on every floor of the house – Jonathan and Jane say they both drink water obsessively while they are at home and want it close at hand. They also buy vast amounts of Diet Coke and Pepsi Max. 'We've probably ingested more aspartame than lab rats,' Jane said once. Their booze cupboard, though, is reserved almost exclusively for dinner guests who often find themselves the only ones drinking as their hosts stick to water and juice. Having said that their last house was the best in England, Jonathan and Jane are determined to repeat the trick this time around as well.

On the career front, the pair had some big decisions to make from the safety of their new home. In 2003, for example, Jonathan's office phone was constantly ringing over the news that Chris Tarrant, one of the long-term kings of radio, was on the point of giving up his daily breakfast show on Capital Radio after some 15 years. Jonathan was widely seen as one of the most likely people to replace him (not least because Chris himself had frequently said what a fan he was of his younger rival) and the station was said to have put together a £3 million, five-year package to try to tempt him.

'Jonathan has a contract with the BBC until next July

and we don't break contracts,' his agent Addison Cresswell said. 'But what happens after that I don't know. We are in discussion with the BBC about his deal now.'

Jonathan was certainly in a strong position to negotiate, should he want to. His Saturday show was attracting a record average of some 3.5 million listeners a week and was well on the way to becoming a broadcasting institution – Jonathan is Terry Wogan in a leopard-print kilt, or a 'post-punk Ronnie Corbett', as one commentator described him.

But was he already bored with the Radio Two routine and prepared for a fresh challenge? In the past, he had said that just two series of a television show were enough to bore the designer pants off him and have him seeking pastures new. But, by 2003, he had, of course, mellowed. He was into his fifth year in the film hot seat and it felt as fresh as ever, and the Saturday-morning radio show still suited him as well. After talking it through with Jane and Addison, Jonathan made his decision on both family and selfish grounds. As he approached his 43rd birthday, he didn't want to have to leave his house at 4.30am to start the 6.00–9.00am breakfast show, missing out in the process on making breakfasts and packed lunches for his children and taking them to school. Those regular domestic tasks were some of his favourite parts of parenthood. No amount of money and no promise of internet-based broadcasting would compensate for giving them up to be on a London-only radio station.

Two other factors helped Jonathan make up his mind and turn down the £3 million job offer. First, he suddenly realised that doing a breakfast show five mornings a week would be just a little bit too close to the full-time job he had spent most of his career trying to avoid. Then there was the fear that defecting from BBC Radio might put some of his BBC television shows in jeopardy. *Friday Night with Jonathan Ross* was secure but, if the powers-that-be were unhappy with him, was there more of a chance that fresh blood might be demanded for *They Think It's All Over*? Or that some of his other one-off shows might not be seen as quite good enough to get the green light any more? It was, perhaps, a risk too far.

Jonathan liked his life in 2003. His family was on an even keel and he didn't want to rock any boats. So, in the end, the Capital job (and what was reported as a far lower salary) went to Johnny Vaughan. Radio Two listeners heaved a big sigh of relief. And, up in Hampstead Garden Suburb, Jonathan got into the habit of listening to Johnny's new show as the family went through its typically boisterous breakfast routines. It had all worked out perfectly, he decided. And, anyway, it was his turn to make some career sacrifices in order to help the family, because Jane was about to enjoy another extended spell in the spotlight.

Her first big job was, of all things, as a lingerie model. Getting her kit off for the boys was hardly something the fiercely feminist, privately educated Jane might have considered doing as recently as a decade earlier. But, by the time the specialist Fantasie bra company approached her, she felt that she, and the times, had changed enough to consider it. Fantasie weren't focusing on the stick-thin women in most other advertising and, by taking part in the campaign, Jane and Jonathan both agreed she was striking a blow for real women with real curves – the kind Jonathan had long since started to favour.

Of course, agreeing to do the work was one thing; seeing her 32F chest on display on massive billboards across the country was another, although Jane had at least retained the right to veto any poses or shots that she didn't want her children to see.

'I'm not exactly going up against Eva Herzigova, because I am older and bigger than most models,' Jane said as the campaign was launched, before letting slip another reason why she was doing it. 'Jonathan is really excited and proud about it all. He pointed out that I wear more revealing outfits on a night out. And now he gets to say that he sleeps with a bra model, which he kind of likes.'

Jane's bigger challenge was putting together a ten-part series for Living TV, however. As her interest in the paranormal and all things connected to it grew, she had become increasingly aware of all the scepticism people felt about the subject – not least in her own home. 'Yeah, yeah, prove it,' Jonathan would say to her, as she talked through yet another theory she had read or been told about. And then they realised that attempting to do so might make fantastic television. After talking to a variety of independent production companies, *Jane Goldman Investigates* was born, with Jane happy to follow in her husband's example by having her own name in a 'does what it says on the tin' programme title.

The idea was inspired by elements of *Faking It* and

developed into a show which delved into the psychic world. Jane and the production team selected ten areas of the supernatural, found the leading experts in each of them, and then gave Jane a month trying to understand or even acquire their skills. It was a major piece of work and Jonathan was happy to hear about it all from the start. 'He has always been sceptical but he is interested in the stories and so catching up on what I've been doing at work means there are some great anecdotes to tell. I guess it is odd for me to come home having been to an animal sacrifice that day. And you do end up having somewhat unusual conversations about what the hell I am supposed to wear to an exorcism,' she says. Jonathan, who sometimes dresses for the school run as if he is going to an exorcism, was always happy to offer his advice.

The first series of the show looked at everything from Tarot card reading, ghosts and astrology to clairvoyance, psychic healing and spell casting. At the start of each show, Jane admitted to her own initial scepticism of the subject under investigation and threw herself into the challenge of proving or disproving it. In the process, everyone had a lot of fun. She spent a day laying hands on penguins with an animal healer, stayed awake all night on ghost vigils and earned certificates in both Reiki healing and Tarot card reading. When it came to investigating reading tealeaves, she started off with the tealeaf reader of the National Tea Council (it really does employ one), and then decided to test the skill on some burly truckers. 'I went to a truck stop in Essex. I reckoned the men would like the tea part at least. I wanted to try it out on people who wouldn't be open to it, but it turned out that they were. I was suddenly having intimate chats with these men, who were saying that they never talked to anyone else like that. It was very moving. And it was very weird when I pointed to specific things in the leaves and one of the blokes said something like that had happened to him that same day.'

Whether or not this was telepathy, mind reading or coincidence, Jane still doesn't know. But she thrived on the challenge of finding out more and explaining it on her show. As the series progressed, she also found a relatively light-hearted way of bringing Jonathan and their old friend David Baddiel into one investigation. 'David always used to complain that he always lost at tennis to Jonathan despite being convinced that he was as good a player,' says Jane. Could she cast a spell on him to remove the 'blocks' in David's mind and make him live up to his potential? She consulted a Glastonbury-based witch, Sally Morningstar, who devised a ritual for her to perform to do just that.

'I spent the day in our garden, building an altar and making my own tools, as all good witches do, then invoking ancient deities and uttering incantations. The result? David lost 6–0, 6–0. So was it the dodgy moon phase that the witch had warned might make the spell ineffective or the pressure of the TV cameras? Or the fact that Jonathan is simply far superior at tennis, as he bragged endlessly?' Again, Jane admitted that she didn't know, but said she was still 'curiously receptive' to the tenets of witchcraft afterwards.

What Jane had also found as she researched the series

was that her audience was to contain several hardcore elements that would be very hard to please. First, there were the general viewers who simply wanted entertainment and, fortunately, she had Jonathan's skills to draw on for advice in keeping her show light enough for them. Then there were the 'knee-jerk critics', people who would slam it purely because of her high profile as Jonathan's wife. She decided she simply had to put them out of her mind. Finally, there were the true supernatural and paranormal fans, most of them members of associations and local groups, who were determined to see their fascinations portrayed properly on screen. Fortunately for Jane, this vital constituency did like what they saw when the show was finally aired. 'There's no beating around the bush with Jane. She's far more level-headed that I had expected, proof that looks can be deceptive,' one wrote on an internet review site.

In terms of ratings, the show was never going to rival any of Jonathan's. But Living TV bosses were happy with the figures it achieved and there were hopes that it might be resold on to a terrestrial channel for a bigger follow-up viewing. Meanwhile, a second series was commissioned for 2004 – and this time Jane made her husband a very happy man by thinking even bigger. The next shows had a different tone. Instead of focusing on Jane being taught by various experts, they investigated the real-life stories of people who claimed to have been affected by paranormal events. Effectively one-hour investigative documentaries, they helped Jane feel she was back in touch with her journalistic roots.

For his part, Jonathan was over the moon because a lot of the work involved some great overseas travel. America, not surprisingly, was the key destination, and Jane went to New England to meet someone who had suffered from poltergeists, to Aspen to meet people who claimed to have seen aliens, and to New Orleans for a show about voodoo ceremonies. Whenever possible, Jonathan and the children came too, sometimes watching Jane at work, sometimes just amusing themselves until her day was over.

The couple's eldest daughter, Betty, was 13 when the second series was being filmed, and she was fascinated by the spooky tales her mother was now able to share with her. But Jane and Jonathan decided to hold some stories back until she was older. The key example was of what happened when Jane and the team were at the Drury Lane Theatre in London investigating a form of 'trans-communication' known as EVP or electronic voice phenomena. It is a form of technology used to try to communicate with the dead and Jane's logical mind said that if any noise came out at all it would only be the sort of static you used to get on radios – or perhaps a burst of voices from a local mini-cab company. As it turned out, there was one very different burst of noise, however, which sounded like human speech – threatening human speech. 'It was a brief sentence... some people hear one thing, others another. And it tied in with something someone said to me earlier, so it was quite portentous,' Jane says. She had taped it on a Dictaphone she had held on her lap but, because no one else had been around her when the sounds came over the system, she was convinced viewers would assume they had been faked. 'It was strange and it was disturbing,' Jane says. And she didn't want Betty to find out about the disembodied voice until she was older.

With the second series in the can and on screen, Jane did find she was winning some long overdue credibility as a professional in her own right. Localised sniping and random innuendo continued in some sections of the media, but a tiny band of reporters seemed finally ready to pay Jonathan's wife her due.

When the pair braved a windy night at the première of a Jim Carrey film, *Lemony Snicket's A Series of Unfortunate Events*, *Daily Mail* fashion writer Shyama Perara finally broke free of her paper's traditional role as Jade Goldman critic-in-chief and gave her a positive review. 'What a gladdening sight she is. A 21st-century woman utterly confident in her own appearance. She is a terrific role model for young women who, in the main, have been bludgeoned into uniformity by dull designers. Into their culture of conformity blows Jane Goldman, whose outlandish wardrobe suggests intellectual humour and emotional confidence,' Perara declared.

Jonathan, meanwhile, was not faring so well. 'He admits that he invented his personal style by copying the fashion of the late 1980s. And the problem is that he's still doing it,' was one review of his latest outfit.

But, as the couple headed home from Leicester Square when the film was over, they at least felt they had turned a corner in the way they were perceived. Life, at last, was looking good.

16

For Services to Broadcasting

You can take the boy out of Leytonstone, but perhaps you can never really take Leytonstone out of the boy. In his diaries, Daily Mirror editor Piers Morgan tells of the Christmas lunch he gave at Mayfair's Mirabelle restaurant for the paper's big-name columnists. Sitting alongside Jonathan were Alan Sugar, Carol Vorderman, Miriam Stoppard and Tony Parsons – a group of some of the very best-paid and most famous people in the entertainment industry. Everyone got scathingly drunk, Piers wrote in his diary, with Jonathan the worst offender.

'On being told the cigars were free, he called over the waiter with the case and helped himself to handfuls of Monte Cristos – stuffing them all into his various pockets. "Cheers, Piers, great fucking party, mate," he cried to general hilarity as he staggered out with his £1,245 haul.'

Psychologists might find easy excuses for Jonathan's behaviour, however. Most say that, when you come from a very poor background, your attitudes to money and possessions, when you finally get them, can be ambivalent to say the least. Jonathan jokes that it took him years to realise that 'disposable income' did not mean income he had to dispose of down the shops as quickly as possible, for example. And he has never been one to keep his good fortune a secret. Back in 1991, he had no problem admitting that he and Jane had mortgages worth £600,000 on their two homes (back then, the average mortgage was just £50,000 according to the Halifax). And, while many would have said he was crazy to take on so much debt back then, the way house prices have soared since proved Jonathan was right to gamble.

On the career front, Chris Evans was the pre-eminent role model of the ordinary boy done particularly good. Jonathan admired the man's honesty at work and his ability to compartmentalise the different roles he played in life. 'I used to let people get away with shoddy work because I didn't want to hurt anyone's feelings and, in the end, we all suffered. Chris showed me how to be tough and that you don't have to have everyone like you all the time. I learned a lot from him, especially how to stand up for myself,' he said. So, with this in mind, he slowly gained a reputation as a confident but fair operator – having learned other lessons from the financially up-front *Weakest Link* presenter Anne Robinson.

'I gradually realised that I was not afraid of talking money with people and I don't equate toughness with not being liked,' Jonathan says. But, before his tough-talking incarnation bedded down, he admits it did sometimes border on the arrogant. 'I am impossible to fire because I am only doing what I do to have fun. I don't need the money. If I shoot a commercial, I can earn what a TV executive earns in a year-and-a-half,' he said when he was having shows and other work thrown at him in the early days of Generation X.

Meanwhile, he was certainly unafraid of surrounding himself with equally money-focused people, even if those people rubbed everyone else up the wrong way. Addison Cresswell, the highly effective, long-term agent and producer who was credited with setting up a lucrative 'comedy mafia' with the likes of Jack Dee, Julian Clary and Lee Evans, was Jonathan's friend as well as his chief negotiator. Yet he hardly had the best of reputations in the industry. 'He's a wanker... a man I would literally cross continents to avoid,' was how then *Mirror* editor Piers Morgan described him after yet another contract negotiation stalled in 2003.

Jonathan was also well aware of the feast or famine nature of the entertainment business. So he tried to be pragmatic about what he did and didn't do. In the first heady *Last Resort* days, he was offered two possible chances to be made a national laughing stock, for example. One was by going on a celebrity edition of *Blind Date*; the other was by taking part in a lager commercial where his voice and clothes were the butt of the joke. He picked the latter – and happily admits it was because it paid him ten times as much money for almost exactly the same amount of work.

The money was always used wisely. For all the jokes

about designer-suit shopping, the boy from Leytonstone was a saver at heart. In his own childhood, he had seen first-hand how important it was even for children to earn money. He knew you could never tell when a rainy day might come or a big financial crisis might hit. He was also aware that the more money he had in the bank, the more power he had to pick which projects to work on and which to refuse. This freedom allowed him to accept far less than his standard going rate in the early days of *Film '99* (though, having said that, he knew when he signed the BBC contract that he could boost the corporation's payments by some related freelancing elsewhere, such as the £75,000 a year he earned writing a film review column for the *Daily Mirror*).

Property is another area where Jonathan and Jane have both scored over the years, following in the footsteps of the vast majority of newly wealthy people in the newspaper's Rich Lists who tend to own far more homes than most ordinary people do. The pair made money out of the first flat Jonathan owned in Shepherd's Bush, the Chalk Farm home they moved into as a married couple and their first huge Hampstead house. Now happily ensconced in their Hampstead Garden Suburb home, Jonathan has discovered one more fantastic way to boost his family finances – by cashing in on the extraordinarily lucrative after-dinner-speaking circuit. Demand for celebrity speakers is huge and, by 2003, when Jonathan was becoming a regular in the market, he was ranked securely among the upper echelon of A-list stars. Experts said he compared favourably in profile with the likes of

Jeremy Clarkson, Stephen Fry, Joanna Lumley, John McEnroe and Sir Trevor McDonald, by being able to collect up to £25,000 for a single speech or a one-off appearance at a product launch or corporate event.

Of course, what he wouldn't promise was that he would be nice to the people paying his inflated wages – which was just what made people love him more. There is a quote from poet and biographer GK Chesterton that says, to succeed with an audience, you need to insult it. Jonathan seemed to have taken the concept at face value. '*Loaded* magazine? It's pornography for losers,' he declared while handing its editor the award for magazine of the year at one glitzy London ceremony he was hosting.

'What people like about having Jonathan talk to their staff is the fact that he would never just provide mindless flattery,' says booker Natasha Stevenson. 'He knows that your average worker secretly likes to take the mickey out of the boss or the company image. And he's ready to do that for them, which normally makes for a fantastic evening – and money well spent in terms of team-building and morale.'

The final piece of the Ross financial jigsaw is made up by the family's Florida home. It has soared in value alongside the booming US economy. But the couple had never bought it to try to make money, and Jonathan, in particular, says that owning it brings benefits that can never be measured in pounds, pence, dollars or cents. From the start, the idea was that it would be the family's refuge from the pace and stress of London life, and it has always delivered.

In 2003, with *It's Only TV But I Like It* cancelled and Jonathan trying to filter out some of the other work he no longer enjoyed, Florida was again the place he and Jane went to for an extended and well-earned rest. They had just spent a huge amount of time and effort pitching a new programme about mad modern artists to the BBC. Jane was to have presented it, and Jonathan's production company, Hot Sauce, would have made it. But, after endless meetings and presentations, the BBC had decided not to commission it. 'We get lots of proposals, we can't take them all and it just wasn't what we are looking for at the moment,' a BBC source told the *Daily Mirror* when the rejection was leaked to the press.

Immediately afterwards, Jonathan and Jane were presented with a potentially lucrative new programme idea from a different channel. Producers apparently reckoned that the Ross family could be the perfect replacements for the Osbournes in a long-running, fly-on-the-wall reality show. Bearing in mind that *The Osbournes* had totally transformed that family's finances, earning them an estimated £17 million in 2002 alone out of the basic programme fee, merchandising and DVD sales, the temptation for the Rosses to follow suit must have been high. But Jonathan and Jane both said 'no' straight away. After so many run-ins with the press in the past, they were determined to protect what was left of their own privacy and, more importantly, to preserve that of their children for as long as possible. If you get into bed with the devil – which was how Jonathan saw the idea of doing a reality-based show – then you have no recourse in the future if you complain about media harassment or intrusion. He wanted to retain that card in case it ever needed to be played in the years ahead. So any future dramas in the Ross household – and deep down everyone hoped there would be very few of them – were destined to take place in private.

Back in Florida, Jonathan ordered a new range of gym equipment to install in the garage of their home so he could kick-start his exercise regime over the family's usual Christmas break. And he had to admit that he needed the new kit, because his other exercise campaigns in the Sunshine State had produced mixed results. 'Roller-blading to the shops in Florida is my least successful exercise,' he says. 'Jane is fine. But the only way I can stand up is to have two kids and a double buggy in front of me and I lean on it all like a Zimmer frame. The kids think it's hilarious, as do all the people who pass by.'

Surfing wasn't something Jonathan took very seriously either. 'I normally take my surfboard across the road very dramatically and seriously and then come straight back saying the waves are too small or something and then just flop back down to channel surf on television,' he admits.

Jane, who admits she had her first cigarette on New Year's Eve when she was 15 and has struggled to give up ever since, says the pair both watch their weight rise and fall in line with their moods. In Florida, Jonathan takes lessons to try to beef up his tennis game for when he comes home, as he plays regularly in the UK with opponents including fellow comedian David Baddiel and Jonathan's Radio Two sparring partner Andy Davies.

While Jonathan takes the mickey out of him endlessly on the show, Tim Henman had become something of a friend after a series of social and charity matches. And, when it comes to producing a new Wimbledon champion, Jonathan has a very un-Henmanesque strategy. 'The toffs are never going to give us any winners. We need to get the commoners on court if we're ever going to produce any really good players. You should hand out tennis rackets at council estates. The kids can hollow out the handles so they've got somewhere to put their crack cocaine as an incentive.'

Also on the fitness front, Jonathan, Jane and old friend Frank Skinner once decided that ice-skating was going to be their sport of choice. Long before ITV had even thought of its 2006 celebrity-fest *Dancing on Ice*, the trio hired a rink for some private lessons. But, after one painful fall too many, they all thought better of it and gave up.

Frank Skinner was one of the tiny band of close confidants who were regular visitors at the Ross house. Vic Reeves and his wife Nancy Sorrell were other famous-name friends. Jane admits that, when too many larger-than-life comedians are all round for dinner, it can be a noisy, raucous affair. 'In private, Jonathan is only slightly quieter than his TV persona, but when we have friends round he can be high-octane, very loud and very amusing. It is exhausting when he has some of his noisiest friends round for dinner as it's a bit like watching *They Think It's All Over* for five straight hours.'

The social high point of the couple's calendar has traditionally been Hallowe'en, when they used to throw wild parties, although now they opt for more child-friendly alternatives.

In a similar vein, a typical night at home for Jonathan and Jane tends to be surprisingly restrained. The couple remain unashamed about loving board games like Scrabble, and they frequently raid the kids' film collections for a lazy night in. 'Sometimes on a Sunday night, one of us will nip down to the offy and buy a whole carrier bag full of chocolate bars. Two of everything – Mars, Bounty, Milky Way, Crunchie, KitKat... We'll watch telly and eat the lot, until we start feeling sick,' says Jane. 'At the same time, we both cry constantly when watching movies, far more than is natural. We both cried six times in *Toy Story 2*, just sitting there clutching each other's hands with tears streaming down our faces.'

Jonathan is the first to admit that his taste in films has broadened over the years – and his whole attitude to life has changed. 'As I've got older and had kids, I've become much softer,' he says. 'I cry much more easily and my buttons are very easily pressed by exploitative filmmakers. I cried when Charlie got the golden ticket in *Charlie and the Chocolate Factory*, and the other day we were all watching *Rugrats* and I got all misty-eyed again. I turned to Jane and said, "I can't believe this... I'm crying at a cartoon!" What does this say about me and my supposed masculinity?'

One thing it did say, of course, was that the comic-loving schoolboy was just as much of a cartoon-lover in adulthood. Over the years, his comic collection had grown alongside his bank balance – he will pay tens of thousands of pounds for rare works by his favourite artists and has found that several of the vintage comics he had bought cheaply many years ago have since soared in value. He also believes that the best modern comics and cartoons are the equal of any other art form – so, in 2003, he was beside himself with excitement when he got the chance to get even closer to the industry.

He had been asked to voice a part in the sequel to the phenomenally successful *Shrek* film. That first animation, made by Steven Spielberg's Dreamworks company, had been a huge international hit back in 2001, and was a favourite with all three of the Ross children. Mike Myers, Eddie Murphy, Cameron Diaz and a host of other Hollywood stars had voiced the main characters and all were being brought back for the follow-up two years later. So was Jonathan finally going to crack America by acting alongside them – albeit in cartoon form?

For a while, it looked as if he was. The part he was to take would cleverly poke fun at his appearance and at his strangely louche image – he would be one of the ugly sisters working as a barmaid at the Poisoned Apple Bar. The first downside was that Jonathan was only going to be heard in the UK version of the film. In the main American and international editions, the ugly sister was being played by chat-show veteran Larry King. The second downside was that Larry's name, rather than Jonathan's, was to be listed even in the UK credits. The third was that Jonathan wasn't heading out to Hollywood to record his words alongside the rest of the stellar cast. In *Shrek 2*, John Cleese and Julie Andrews apparently broke cartoon convention by recording their scenes together, but the remaining voices were all recorded individually, as is the case in most animations. Jonathan didn't even have to leave London to get his voice on tape, though he did, of course, meet up with each of the film's main stars when he later interviewed them on *Film 2004*.

And, when *Shrek 2* was released in 2004, it was another huge hit. In Britain, where we got to hear Jonathan's voice (and Kate Thornton's, who had been drafted in to replace Joan Rivers), it made £16 million in its first three days on release, in the process knocking *Harry Potter and the Prisoner of Azkaban* off the top spot in the box office. The entire Ross family went to the West End première while Jonathan joked about preparing an 'I'd like to thank the Academy...' speech for his fictional Best Supporting Cartoon Actor category. Even in his dreams, though, he said Larry King somehow managed to upstage him and grab most of the glory.

While Hollywood hadn't exactly been beating a path to Jonathan's door after his role in *Shrek 2*, Jonathan was in line for one other high-profile phone call the following year. It was from Buckingham Palace.

An official letter confirmed the news, although Jonathan wasn't able to tell a soul until the announcement was made that June – he was to be awarded an OBE for 'Services to Broadcasting' in the Queen's Birthday Honours list. Jonathan's public statement said he was 'delighted and proud' at the news. In private, he was ecstatic, and surprisingly emotional. Always fiercely patriotic, he was a huge believer in the traditions and structures that made Britain different to his equally beloved America. This sort of personal recognition from the Queen was incredibly humbling. The message he wanted to get across, he said, was that, even if you are brought up five to a room in rough old Leytonstone, then hard work and commitment can still take you anywhere you want to go. He thought the OBE, in effect, said as much about Britain as it did about his own achievements, and that made him proud and patriotic in equal measure.

Sitting at home with his wife and family as his agent fielded calls for interviews about the honour, Jonathan was equally aware of the long road he had taken to get to this point. As such a rich and successful broadcaster in 2005, it was easy to forget how many hurdles he had overcome at the start of his career some 18 years earlier – and how important he had been in opening media doors to other people who don't have perfect enunciation or standard accents. Being awarded a 'Services to Broadcasting' OBE meant Jonathan was in pretty good company – especially among his peers on radio. Terry Wogan had been given the same honour back in 1997; Jimmy Young had got the OBE in 2001 alongside *Woman's Hour* veteran Jenni Murray; while John Peel and *Last of the Summer Wine* creator Roy Clarke had got similar commendations just before Jonathan. On the wider Birthday Honours list of 2005, Jonathan found himself alongside David Jason, who was knighted, and Dame Judi Dench, who became a Companion of Honour, a select band comprising just 65 individuals recognised for being of 'national importance'.

While the announcement of the Birthday Honours list is always made in June, the awards themselves are not presented until later in the year. Jonathan's turn came in November when he arrived at Buckingham Palace for the ceremony. Everyone being honoured is allowed to invite up to three guests to witness the occasion, and Jonathan was there with Jane and his parents.

Contrary to most people's expectations, Jonathan was particularly soberly dressed that day, in a restrained dark-grey suit. It had been a deliberate decision, though, as usual, Jonathan was ready to make a bit of a joke about it. 'I thought it would be easy to go the flamboyant route but, for once, I didn't want to offend anybody. And, anyway, I also thought of how good David Beckham looked in the traditional stuff when he got his so I thought I would try and be him rather than me for a day.' And, of course, Jonathan did sneak in at least one individual touch – a slender cane with a small silver skull on the handle.

His other plan was to shake up the photo call by holding up his medal alongside his other Establishment treasure, a phoney *Blue Peter* badge he had been sent as a boy, but he failed to achieve this when he realised he had left the 30-year-old badge in the car.

During the investiture ceremony itself, carried out by Prince Charles, whom Jonathan had met several times at charity events, Jonathan says his unexpected nerves caused him to make a weak joke. 'It's not too late to take this back, you know,' he told the Prince as the cross was about to be pinned to his chest. For his part, Prince Charles simply smiled, and showed he was more in touch with popular culture than many people might imagine. 'Charles said, "I don't know how you manage to fit them all in," about my shows,' beamed Jonathan afterwards. It was proof that even the royals must watch and listen to him – another big confidence booster for the boy from Leytonstone.

After the ceremony in Buckingham Palace's Ballroom, Jonathan was given another reminder of how far he had travelled in life – quite literally. Also being honoured on the same day was Sir Rod Eddington, the departing boss of British Airways. As one of the airline's most frequent Business and First Class flyers, Jonathan had plenty to say to the man who ran the company. Of the other guests that day, he says meeting 1960s Blues legend John Mayall was another thrill. 'A wonderful day... a magical, wonderful day,' was all he kept saying to reporters as he headed off to find Jane and his parents and left the Palace for a celebratory lunch in the West End. Throughout it, Jonathan says he simply couldn't stop smiling and practically had to resort to the cliché of pinching himself to check it wasn't a dream.

Part of Jonathan's long-term charm is his sheer love of life and his near childlike lack of cynicism. World-weary is never going to be a fair description of his state of mind. He craves new life-affirming experiences and values the memories of every high and low. For all the jokes and the comedy, he saw being awarded an OBE as a serious business and he was seriously proud of it. Not, of course, that he would always show it. He celebrated the event by playing the Sex Pistols' 'God Save the Queen' as the first song on his next Radio Two show – and, by this time, the carping at his award had already begun.

The *Mail on Sunday* dubbed the award 'a disgrace' and a line of critics were also preparing to speak out against it. David Turtle of the independent broadcasting watchdog Mediawatch said giving an OBE to Jonathan set 'an appalling example to children' by appearing to endorse offensive remarks and swearing. 'Who decides the recipients of these things?' Turtle asked of the awards. 'It is absurd. He is best known for showering the airwaves with expletives, which is hardly something we should be encouraging.'

In a terrible piece of bad timing, Turtle did in some ways seem to have a point. *Friday Night with Jonathan Ross* was still racking up more than its fair share of complaints from viewers. Just before Jonathan had been named on the Birthday Honours list, the BBC had been forced to issue a rare official apology when 350 viewers complained about comments made by Jonathan's guest Marc Wootton. Wootton was playing the role of spoof 'psychic-to-the-stars' Shirley Ghostman and the complainants said they thought his remarks were, among many other things, anti-Semitic and offensive. 'The spoof nature of this character was perhaps unclear to some viewers,' admitted the BBC after Jonathan and his producers' knuckles were once more given a subtle rap behind the scenes.

Heading back home after the big day and reunited in the car with his *Blue Peter* badge, Jonathan and Jane took another close look at the OBE itself. The silver cross, with its soft red ribbon, is set in a simple black box. Ornate and detailed close up, it obviously fits easily in the palm of your hand. And Jonathan had to admit that, while this was perhaps the most important award he had ever won, it was just as well that it didn't take up much space because, back at home, his awards' cabinet was already creaking with the kind of heavyweight silverware that would put José Mourinho to shame.

Among many other major awards, he had won a Royal Television Society Award for Best Entertainment Performance, a Broadcast award for Best Light Entertainment Programme, a British Comedy Award, and Television & Radio Industries Club Awards for Radio Personality of the Year and Television Personality of the Year – in the same year. He collected two Baftas in 2004, including the Lew Grade Award for Entertainment Programme or Series and has won several 'viewer-voted' awards as well, accolades he says that mean as much if not more to him as those awarded by his peers in the industry. Endearingly enough, he also says that being named Dad of the Year by the Early Learning Centre in 2004 had meant as much to him as any of his professionally earned gongs. And he also joked that the Early Learning award had given him a lot of extra help at home. 'I'm Dad of the Year. So you have to do what I tell you,' became his temporary new mantra with the kids. Though, when 14-year-old Betty proved that she had inherited her father's quick wit by telling him she had voted for someone else, he was uncharacteristically lost for words.

What Jonathan was increasingly proud of that

summer was how well his three childr
up. He and Jane had both been surpr
good behaviour, especially in public,
been very young. And it seemed to be paying o..
life still had downs as well as ups but, in general, the
Ross clan seemed incredibly comfortable together. And
Jane and Jonathan seemed to be going through an
extended happy honeymoon period some 18 years after
they had first met. Former rival and role model Chris
Evans was one of the first to put it into words. 'There
are very few people you meet in the world and think,
"They are it." But Jonathan and Jane are "it".
Completely and totally devoted to each other,' he
explained in a rare moment of seriousness.

Jane says Jonathan has always been a lot more romantic
than most people realise – she says the songs he dedicates
to her on his Radio Two show are just one way he has
found to show it. 'It's not about sending flowers, although
they are nice. What I call romance is to do with
thoughtfulness and Jonathan does things which are
genuinely thoughtful, done because they are totally meant.
Leaving me little notes, buying little presents as a surprise,
just because he sees them in a shop and thinks I may like
them. Or bringing me breakfast in bed or making the
house look wonderful if I come home later than him one
evening. That's what makes me think I've got the best
husband in the world.'

For his part, Jonathan felt he was the happiest husband.
He and Jane had both been shocked to the core in the past
few years when both their parents had split up after what

everyone had thought were rock-solid relationships. But they still couldn't imagine the same happening to them. 'I am not just a happily married man... I am a very happily married man,' Jonathan said. 'And the longer we stay together, the better it is. The main thing we try to remember is that we are with each other through choice and because we want to be.'

What helped the couple was the very private world they had created for each other, the long-term heritage of shared memories, moments, interests and jokes. Who other than Jane, for example, might have guessed that her trivia and popular culture-loving husband wanted something as serious and grown-up as a first edition by Vladimir Nabokov, the Russian author of *Lolita*, for his 40th birthday? Often, the couple were convinced that they really could read each other's mind. They said they could always state with absolute certainty what the other's opinions would be on any given subject. And, for all the occasional seriousness, they were also prepared to act like kids when it suited them. 'We often stop and say, "God, if anyone saw us or heard us they would just be absolutely horrified,"' says Jane. 'We tell each other really childish jokes about bodily functions and we make up utterly stupid songs. I'm not sure I can think of anyone else we could do that with, which is why it's so great that we found each other.'

As the family bonds grew tighter, Jonathan and Jane decided to try to put down some other roots elsewhere. In the summer of 2005, after some two years of looking, they settled upon a 16th-century farmhouse near

Swanage on the Dorset coast. It was far enough from London to give the family the sense that they had escaped the city, but close enough for impromptu weekends or even the occasional evening outing. It was also private. There is a big caravan park near by, on the way to the nudist beach at Studland Bay, but the house itself has nearly six acres of grounds – in which there is a swimming pool in a converted barn. Most importantly for the children are the stables in the farm's orchard. All three are following their mum's example and becoming keen and increasingly fearless riders, so the chance to have their own horses in the back garden one day was a major reason why their parents forked out the £1.1 million needed for the Grade II listed property. As second homes go, it was impressive stuff.

'We're pretty quiet, we don't go out a lot, or drink, so we don't go crazy. But it's never boring,' is how Jane describes their life in town as well as in the country. But, whichever home they are in, there is always plenty going on – because, as well as the three children, Jonathan and Jane share their lives with a bizarre menagerie of pets. Over the years, many have come and gone (frequently buried in the back of the north London garden after quiet moving ceremonies). But, as well as the standard cats and dogs, the less usual furry (and scaly) friends have included chinchillas, six ferrets, a rabbit, a pair of iguanas, a snake, a pair of salamanders and a whole host of newts. Chickens and guinea pigs live in vast hutches and the family rebuilt an old aviary at their Hampstead Garden Suburb house. Jonathan even adopted an ape called

Seamus at Monkey World near Wool in Dorset, though the children were upset when they found out that this didn't mean Seamus could ever come and stay with them at weekends.

Not even the animals are safe from his occasional jokes, though. When one of the iguanas, Blossom, had to be given away because she didn't get on with Dave (the female iguana that the family had wrongly assumed was male), Jonathan couldn't resist winding pet-lovers up. 'I'm wearing her,' he said, pointing to his shoes one day and winking.

One key thing which keeps his and Jane's relationship strong, now their past problems are relegated to the history books, is that their careers allow them to spend a lot of quality time together. Jonathan may seem as if he is constantly on television, but many of his shows are filmed in short concentrated bursts of activity. He writes his scripts and does much of his research from home. He watches films for his reviews in his flash new study, and he goes out far less frequently in the evening than you might imagine. And, when he does, it is often with Jane at his side.

It all means that, unlike many professional couples who suddenly realise they have turned into strangers after too many long days and late nights at separate offices, the Rosses continue to know each other intimately and they thrive off that knowledge. Despite the twin divorces of their parents, they also remain close to their families, which, for Jonathan in particular, means Christmas is a very busy time. His mother Martha normally tries to gather the entire Ross clan – now around 40-strong – for a series of big events. The first is often a mass visit to a pantomime, normally one produced by husband Tony's OK Theatre Company. The Sunday before the big day itself, Martha then throws another huge party, often now in a rented hall in north-east London, because there are too many people to fit into her Essex house. 'We have karaoke where the kids like to sing all the latest hits and we adults sing "White Christmas" and "Have Yourself a Merry Little Christmas". The whole family likes making noise. You should try shutting us up,' she says, unwittingly explaining once again how her entire brood ended up in the entertainment industry.

Immediately after Martha's big parties, Jonathan, Jane and their children normally fly out to Florida for the big day itself – they traditionally celebrate with lobster instead of turkey and spend the afternoon on the beach. But, when they spend Christmas in London instead, they don't believe in making life any harder than it need be. 'The last time I spent Christmas with Jonathan, he and Jane had ordered a turkey from Prince Charles's Duchy Originals and it was fantastic. All the roast potatoes, vegetables and even the Christmas pudding were delivered on Christmas Eve, ready to cook,' his mum says.

When it comes to presents, the emphasis is on fun rather than finance. Martha says she spends all year picking up a present idea here and there for her children and grandchildren – and loves taking the mickey out of her sons. 'I always try and get Jonathan and Paul something funny. When they were little, they used to hoot with laughter over an advertisement showing a man with nasal hair. Well, now they are old men, they could find a trimmer in their sacks themselves this year,' she laughs. Other gifts have been equally well thought out over the years, and entirely reflect Jonathan's unique tastes. His mum recently bought him a mosaic candleholder and a leopardskin magazine rack. 'I also like to get Jonathan musical things and wind-up robots, because he is still just a big kid.'

For his part, Jonathan goes 'off list' when buying for his mum. All she ever asks for is updated photos of her grandchildren. But, for Christmas 2005, he bought her a handbag and some new gloves and a scarf for cold days on the set at *EastEnders* where she still works. He and Jane spent the next few months sitting at home on weekday evenings trying to spot them on screen.

As they did so, they had plenty of opportunities to see trailers for a selection of Jonathan's new shows. In 2006, after having earned his own show on radio, becoming the nation's most authoritative TV film critic, pulling in mass audiences for his chat show on Friday nights and appearing on almost every comedy panel show on TV, Jonathan was ready to branch out into some far more esoteric genres. He was happy to admit that his regular work didn't just keep his bank balance looking good; it also allowed him to take the safety net away and walk along a different career tightrope. He could balance the popular and the populist shows with more offbeat alternatives – shows he desperately wanted to make, even if their audiences would be measured in the thousands rather than the millions.

In early 2006, for example, he was more than happy to be a rare big name on the fledgling BBC4 channel, which screened *Jonathan Ross's Asian Invasion*. From the very start, this was to be no mere 'cut and paste' review programme with a 'talking-head-for-hire' host drafted in to read someone else's script. Instead, it was Jonathan's personal passion and, from the very start, he put a huge number of hours into the project. 'I was astonished by the "hit ratio" of Korean film,' he said of the initial research process – though, again, he couldn't resist throwing in a quick quip as he explained more. 'Whereas I might be truly impressed by about a dozen out of every hundred interesting-looking films I view, the Korean pile yielded several times that. These guys "get" cinema the way the French "get" food, the Italians "get" clothes and the Americans "get" cluelessness.'

Another one-off show, this time on the equally fringe BBC3, also gave Jonathan the chance to get something else out of his system – his long-dormant love of punk rock. As a teenager in Leytonstone, one too many punk gigs had caused him to do so badly in his O levels that he had needed to retake them. Three decades later, it was time to take a new look at the whole era and the role punk had played in it.

In the documentary, *1-2 FU*, Jonathan was determined not to follow the kind of pattern you might expect on an arm's length *South Bank Show* investigation. Instead, he picked out a retro T-shirt and jacket (complete with safety pins), got himself a near-Mohican spikey haircut (a wig), and joined Captain Sensible and two dozen other punks on an open-top bus tour around the old punk haunts of London. The show, billed with total honesty as 'the memories of a middle-aged punk', examined the rise and ultimate demise of the punk era. While viewing figures were tiny, those who watched said the whole thing was as surreal as it sounds, especially at the end when Jonathan joined fellow 40-something fan Vic Reeves in a one-night-only gig where they sang as The Fat Punks. And had a blast.

On a more serious note, Jonathan found he had somehow acquired a certain cultural gravitas. When the reclusive comic artist Alan Moore was profiled on BBC2's *The Culture Show* in 2006, Jonathan was one of the first people the producers wanted to interview about him. The boy from Leytonstone was known as one of the country's biggest comic collectors, and a man whose knowledge of the art form was hard to beat.

Jonathan has also developed a huge interest in film posters – both modern and classic – and he is building up quite a collection of those as well. Experts say he has also become one of the biggest buyers of Japanese model robots and he is quietly building a reputation as one of the country's foremost experts on them as well.

What makes Jonathan's life so enviable is the fact that he can now mix his hobbies and the fun low-budget stuff such as *1-2 FU* with the glitzy excesses that come with being so close to the very top of the entertainment tree. So far, he has never been inside the Kodak Theater itself for the Oscar ceremony. But he regularly goes to LA to commentate on the show, even if this leads to a rare moment of sartorial disappointment. 'It's gutting. I spend months preparing my outfit and then I get there and all anyone wants to do is take pictures of Nicole Kidman and Julia Roberts. Sometimes I wonder why I bother,' he joked after his most recent American adventure.

One reason why he bothered, though, was that he needed to keep his unrivalled contact book alive. While *Crash*, *Capote* and *Brokeback Mountain* were slugging it out for the 2006 Academy Awards, Jonathan was preparing for a new series of *Hollywood Greats* for BBC1 – his first subject was Harrison Ford and Jonathan wanted to make sure he had several other A-list stars lined up for the future.

As that series prepared to launch in early April, he and Jane both had new challenges to face. Jane was putting the finishing touches to the proofs of *Dreamworld II*, the long-awaited sequel to her first Florida-based novel – and there was talk of simultaneously turning the original book into a television show or even a film. She was also putting in the hours to try to get a different film made – *Stardust*, which she had co-written with *Lock, Stock and Two Smoking Barrels* producer Matthew Vaughan.

Jonathan, meanwhile, had finally decided to give his workload a spring clean. After seven years and 16 series, he was giving up his role on *They Think It's All Over*, joking with reporters, 'It's a fantastic show and, from now on, I will be able to watch it. I have had a great time imparting my vast sporting knowledge to the nation.' In place of that panel show, Jonathan took friendly revenge on Mark Lamarr by taking a more frequent role as guest host of *Never Mind the Buzzcocks*. It was a total turnaround from the bad old days of the late 1990s when Jonathan's sole role on the show seemed to have been as the butt of Mark's jokes. Nearly a decade later, the critics loved the way Jonathan hit the ground running on his first night in charge. 'Laugh-out-loud irreverence – how he gets away with it is anyone's guess. Ross says things few others would be allowed to do, excusing his excesses with that familiar cheeky grin and a knowing glance at the camera,' said the *Mirror* of his initial performance. For his part, Jonathan said he simply liked the chance to work with the *Buzzcocks*' production team, he liked the guests on the show and he felt more comfortable joking about music rather than sport.

What he also knew was that for every good review about a show like *Never Mind the Buzzcocks*, there would be a grim one about something else waiting in the wings. So he wasn't expecting an easy ride as he prepared for the tenth series of *Friday Night with Jonathan Ross* – and he certainly didn't get one. 'Wossie's ego-a-thon rumbles on. Ant and Dec and the other guests will struggle to get a word in edgeways and, to be honest, you wonder why they bother. As usual, the only thing that Wossie is really going to want to talk about is himself. Ten series too many,' was how one paper put it as the cameras prepared to roll.

Once upon a time, that kind of comment would have preyed on Jonathan's mind for days. Now it is water off a duck's back. The shy short-sighted comic-lover from Leytonstone has already come a long way and learned just how to put his showbusiness life into proper perspective. Yes, there are a lot more shows he wants to make. Yes, he still dreams of beating Barry Norman's 26-year record in the BBC's cinema hot seat. But his primary ambitions now have nothing to do with television, radio or film. Instead, he says his priority is simply to keep his children safe and to see them grow into happy, well-balanced adults.

When he looks at his awards cabinet, Jonathan Ross sees his OBE, his Baftas and all his comedy gongs. But still says his Dad of the Year award from the Early Learning Centre means more to him than all the others put together. And that, for once, is no joke.